IMPERIALISM
THE HIGHEST STAGE OF CAPITALISM

Imperialism

THE HIGHEST STAGE OF CAPITALISM

A POPULAR OUTLINE

V. I. Lenin

INTERNATIONAL PUBLISHERS

NEW YORK

John Roberts

CONTENTS

Preface to the Russian Edition

The pamphlet here presented to the reader was written in Zürich in the spring of 1916. In the conditions in which I was obliged to work there I naturally suffered somewhat from a shortage of French and English literature and from a serious dearth of Russian literature. However, I made use of the principal English work, *Imperialism*, J. A. Hobson's book, with all the care that, in my opinion, that work deserves.

This pamphlet was written with an eye to the tsarist censorship. Hence, I was not only forced to confine myself strictly to an exclusively theoretical, mainly economic analysis of facts, but to formulate the few necessary observations on politics with extreme caution, by hints, in that Æsopian language—in that cursed Æsopian language—to which tsarism compelled all revolutionaries to have recourse whenever they took up their pens to write a "legal" work.[1]

It is very painful, in these days of liberty, to read these cramped passages of the pamphlet, crushed, as they seem, in an iron vise, distorted on account of the censor. Of how imperialism is the eve of the socialist revolution; of how social-chauvinism (socialism in words, chauvinism in deeds) is the utter betrayal of socialism, complete desertion to the side of the bourgeoisie; of how the split in the labour movement is bound up with the objective conditions of imperialism, etc., I had to speak in a "slavish" tongue, and I must refer the reader who is interested in the question to the volume, which is soon to appear, in which are reproduced the articles I wrote abroad in the years 1914-17. Special attention must be drawn, however, to a passage on pages 119-20.[2] In order to show, in a guise acceptable to the censors, how shamefully the

---

[1] "Æsopian," after the Greek fable writer Æsop, was the term applied to the allusive and roundabout style adopted in "legal" publications by revolutionaries in order to evade the censorship.—*Ed.*

[2] *Cf.* pp. 121-22 in this volume.—*Ed.*

capitalists and the social-chauvinist deserters (whom Kautsky opposes with so much inconsistency) lie on the question of annexations; in order to show with what cynicism they *screen* the annexations of *their* capitalists, I was forced to quote as an example —Japan! The careful reader will easily substitute Russia for Japan, and Finland, Poland, Courland, the Ukraine, Khiva, Bokhara, Estonia or other regions peopled by non-Great Russians, for Korea.

I trust that this pamphlet will help the reader to understand the fundamental economic question, *viz.,* the question of the economic essence of imperialism, for unless this is studied, it will be impossible to understand and appraise modern war and modern politics

Petrograd, April 26, 1917

Preface to the French and German Editions

I

As was indicated in the preface to the Russian edition, this pamphlet was written in 1916, with an eye to the tsarist censorship. I am unable to revise the whole text at the present time, nor, perhaps, is this advisable, since the main purpose of the book was and remains: to present, on the basis of the summarised returns of irrefutable bourgeois statistics, and the admissions of bourgeois scholars of all countries, a *general picture* of the world capitalist system in its international relationships at the beginning of the twentieth century—on the eve of the first world imperialist war.

To a certain extent it will be useful for many Communists in advanced capitalist countries to convince themselves by the example of this pamphlet, *legal, from the standpoint of the tsarist censor,* of the possibility—and necessity—of making use of even the slight remnants of legality which still remain at the disposal of the Communists, say, in contemporary America or France, after the recent wholesale arrests of Communists, in order to explain the utter falsity of social-pacifist views and hopes for "world democracy." The most essential of what should be added to this censored pamphlet I shall try to present in this preface.

II

In the pamphlet I proved that the war of 1914-18 was imperialistic (that is, an annexationist, predatory, plunderous war) on the part of both sides; it was a war for the division of the world, for the partition and repartition of colonies, "spheres of influence" of finance capital, etc.

Proof of what was the true social, or rather, the true class character of the war is naturally to be found, not in the diplomatic history of the war, but in an analysis of the *objective* position of the ruling *classes in all* belligerent countries. In order to depict this objective position one must not take examples or isolated data

(in view of the extreme complexity of social life it is always quite
easy to select any number of examples or separate data to prove
any point one desires), but the *whole* of the data concerning the
basis of economic life in *all* the belligerent countries and the *whole*
world.

It is precisely irrefutable summarised data of this kind that I
quoted in describing the *partition of the world* in the period of
1876 to 1914 (in chapter VI) and the distribution of the *railways*
all over the world in the period of 1890 to 1913 (in chapter VII).
Railways combine within themselves the basic capitalist industries:
coal, iron and steel; and they are the most striking index of the
development of international trade and bourgeois-democratic civilisation. In the preceding chapters of the book I showed how the
railways are linked up with large-scale industry, with monopolies,
syndicates, cartels, trusts, banks and the financial oligarchy. The
uneven distribution of the railways, their uneven development—
sums up, as it were, modern world monopolist capitalism. And
this summing up proves that imperialist wars are absolutely inevitable under *such* an economic system, *as long as* private property
in the means of production exists.

The building of railways seems to be a simple, natural, democratic, cultural and civilising enterprise; that is what it is in the
opinion of bourgeois professors, who are paid to depict capitalist
slavery in bright colours, and in the opinion of petty-bourgeois
philistines. But as a matter of fact the capitalist threads, which
in thousands of different intercrossings bind these enterprises with
private property in the means of production in general, have converted this work of construction into an instrument for oppressing
a thousand million people (in the colonies and semi-colonies), that
is, more than half the population of the globe, which inhabits the
subject countries, as well as the wage slaves of capitalism in the
lands of "civilisation."

Private property based on the labour of the small proprietor, free
competition, democracy, *i.e.,* all the catchwords with which the
capitalists and their press deceive the workers and the peasants—
are things of the past. Capitalism has grown into a world system
of colonial oppression and of the financial strangulation of the

overwhelming majority of the people of the world by a handful of "advanced" countries. And this "booty" is shared between two or three powerful world marauders armed to the teeth (America, Great Britain, Japan), who involve the whole world in *their* war over the sharing of *their* booty.

III

The Brest-Litovsk Peace Treaty dictated by monarchist Germany, and later on, the much more brutal and despicable Versailles Treaty dictated by the "democratic" republics of America and France and also by "free" England, have rendered very good service to humanity by exposing both the hired coolies of the pen of imperialism and the petty-bourgeois reactionaries, although they call themselves pacifists and socialists, who sang praises to "Wilsonism," and who insisted that peace and reform were possible under imperialism.

The tens of millions of dead and maimed left by the war—a war for the purpose of deciding whether the British or German group of financial marauders is to receive the lion's share—and the two "peace treaties," mentioned above, open the eyes of the millions and tens of millions of people who are downtrodden, oppressed, deceived and duped by the bourgeoisie with unprecedented rapidity. Thus, out of the universal ruin caused by the war a worldwide revolutionary crisis is arising which, in spite of the protracted and difficult stages it may have to pass, cannot end in any other way than in a proletarian revolution and in its victory.

The Basle Manifesto of the Second International which in 1912 gave an appraisal of the war that ultimately broke out in 1914, and not of war in general (there are all kinds of wars, including revolutionary wars), this Manifesto is now a monument exposing the shameful bankruptcy and treachery of the heroes of the Second International.

That is why I reproduce this Manifesto as a supplement to the present edition [1] and again I call upon the reader to note that the

[1] *Cf.* V. I. Lenin, *The Imperialist War,* Collected Works, Vol. XVIII, N. Y., pp. 468-72.—*Ed.*

heroes of the Second International are just as assiduously avoiding the passages of this Manifesto which speak precisely, clearly and definitely of the connection between that impending war and the proletarian revolution, as a thief avoids the place where he has committed a theft.

IV

Special attention has been devoted in this pamphlet to a criticism of "Kautskyism," the international ideological trend represented in all countries of the world by the "prominent theoreticians" and leaders of the Second International (Otto Bauer and Co. in Austria, Ramsay MacDonald and others in England, Albert Thomas in France, etc., etc.) and multitudes of socialists, reformists, pacifists, bourgeois-democrats and parsons.

This ideological trend is, on the one hand, a product of the disintegration and decay of the Second International, and, on the other hand, it is the inevitable fruit of the ideology of the petty bourgeoisie, who, by the whole of their conditions of life, are held captive to bourgeois and democratic prejudices.

The views held by Kautsky and his like are a complete renunciation of the very revolutionary principles of Marxism which he championed for decades, especially in his struggle against socialist opportunism (Bernstein, Millerand, Hyndman, Gompers, etc.). It is not a mere accident, therefore, that the "Kautskyans" all over the world have now united in practical politics with the extreme opportunists (through the Second, or the Yellow, International) and with the bourgeois governments (through bourgeois coalition governments in which socialists take part).

The growing world proletarian revolutionary movement in general, and the Communist movement in particular, demands that the theoretical errors of "Kautskyism" be analysed and exposed. The more so since pacifism and "democracy" in general, which have no claim to Marxism whatever, but which, like Kautsky and Co., are obscuring the profundity of the contradictions of imperialism and the inevitable revolutionary crisis to which it gives rise, are still very widespread all over the world. It is the bounden duty of the party of the proletariat to combat these tendencies and to win away from the bourgeoisie the small proprietors who are duped by them, and the millions of toilers who live in more or less petty-bourgeois conditions of life.

V

A few words must be said about chapter VIII entitled: "The Parasitism and Decay of Capitalism." As already pointed out in the text, Hilferding, ex-Marxist, and now a comrade-in-arms of Kautsky, one of the chief exponents of bourgeois reformist policy in the Independent Social-Democratic Party of Germany, has taken a step backward compared with the *frankly* pacifist and reformist Englishman, Hobson, on this question. The international split of the whole labour movement is now quite evident (Second and Third Internationals). Armed struggle and civil war between the two trends is now a recognised fact: the support given to Kolchak and Denikin in Russia by the Mensheviks and Socialist-Revolutionaries against the Bolsheviks; the fight the Scheidemanns, Noskes and Co. have conducted in conjunction with the bourgeoisie against the Spartacists in Germany; the same thing in Finland, Poland, Hungary, etc. What is the economic basis of this historically important world phenomenon?

Precisely the parasitism and decay of capitalism which are the characteristic features of its highest historical stage of development, *i.e.,* imperialism. As has been shown in this pamphlet, capitalism has now brought to the front a *handful* (less than one-tenth of the inhabitants of the globe; less than one-fifth, if the most "generous" and liberal calculations were made) of very rich and very powerful states which plunder the whole world simply by "clipping coupons." Capital exports produce an income of eight to ten billion francs per annum, according to pre-war prices and pre-war bourgeois statistics. Now, of course, they produce much more than that.

Obviously, out of such enormous *super-profits* (since they are obtained over and above the profits which capitalists squeeze out of the workers of their "home" country) it is quite *possible to bribe* the labour leaders and the upper stratum of the labour aristocracy.

And the capitalists of the "advanced" countries are bribing them; they bribe them in a thousand different ways, direct and indirect, overt and covert.

This stratum of bourgeoisified workers, or the "labour aristocracy," who are quite philistine in their mode of life, in the size of their earnings and in their outlook, serves as the principal prop of the Second International, and, in our days, the principal *social* (not military) *prop of the bourgeoisie*. They are the real *agents of the bourgeoisie in the labour movement,* the labour lieutenants of the capitalist class, real channels of reformism and chauvinism. In the civil war between the proletariat and the bourgeoisie they inevitably, and in no small numbers, stand side by side with the bourgeoisie, with the "Versaillese" against the "Communards."

Not the slightest progress can be made toward the solution of the practical problems of the Communist movement and of the impending social revolution unless the economic roots of this phenomenon are understood and unless its political and sociological significance is appreciated.

Imperialism is the eve of the proletarian social revolution. This has been confirmed since 1917 on a world-wide scale.

N. LENIN

July 6, 1920

Imperialism, the Highest Stage of Capitalism

During the last fifteen or twenty years, especially since the Spanish-American War (1898), and the Anglo-Boer War (1899-1902), the economic and also the political literature of the two hemispheres has more and more often adopted the term "imperialism" in order to define the present era. In 1902, a book by the English economist, J. A. Hobson, *Imperialism,* was published in London and New York. This author, who adopts the point of view of bourgeois social reformism and pacifism which, in essence, is identical with the present point of view of the ex-Marxist, K. Kautsky, gives an excellent and comprehensive description of the principal economic and political characteristics of imperialism. In 1910, there appeared in Vienna the work of the Austrian Marxist, Rudolf Hilferding, *Finance Capital.* In spite of the mistake the author commits on the theory of money, and in spite of a certain inclination on his part to reconcile Marxism with opportunism, this work gives a very valuable theoretical analysis, as its sub-title tells us, of "the latest phase of capitalist development." Indeed, what has been said of imperialism during the last few years, especially in a great many magazine and newspaper articles, and also in the resolutions, for example, of the Chemnitz and Basle Congresses which took place in the autumn of 1912, has scarcely gone beyond the ideas put forward, or, more exactly, summed up by the two writers mentioned above.

Later on we shall try to show briefly, and as simply as possible, the connection and relationships between the *principal* economic features of imperialism. We shall not be able to deal with non-economic aspects of the question, however much they deserve to be dealt with.[1] We have put references to literature and other notes which, perhaps, would not interest all readers, at the end of this pamphlet.[2]

[1] By "non-economic" Lenin meant political; the pamphlet was intended for legal publication and so these aspects were left out in order to enable it to pass the tsarist censorship.—*Ed.*

[2] These references are not given in this edition.—*Ed.*

CHAPTER I

Concentration of Production
and Monopolies

THE enormous growth of industry and the remarkably rapid process of concentration of production in ever-larger enterprises represent one of the most characteristic features of capitalism. Modern censuses of production give very complete and exact data on this process.

In Germany, for example, for every 1,000 industrial enterprises, large enterprises, *i.e.*, those employing more than 50 workers, numbered three in 1882, six in 1895 and nine in 1907; and out of every 100 workers employed, this group of enterprises employed 22, 30 and 37 respectively. Concentration of production, however, is much more intense than the concentration of workers, since labour in the large enterprises is much more productive. This is shown by the figures available on steam engines and electric motors. If we take what in Germany is called industry in the broad sense of the term, that is, including commerce, transport, etc., we get the following picture: Large-scale enterprises: 30,588 out of a total of 3,265,623, that is to say, 0.9 per cent. These large-scale enterprises employ 5,700,000 workers out of a total of 14,400,000, that is, 39.4 per cent; they use 6,660,000 steam horse power out of a total of 8,800,000, that is, 75.3 per cent and 1,200,000 kilowatts of electricity out of a total of 1,500,000, that is, 77.2 per cent.

Less than one-hundredth of the total enterprises utilise *more than three-fourths* of the steam and electric power! Two million nine hundred and seventy thousand small enterprises (employing up to five workers), representing 91 per cent of the total, utilise only 7 per cent of the steam and electric power. Tens of thousands of large-scale enterprises are everything; millions of small ones are nothing.

In 1907, there were in Germany 586 establishments employing

one thousand and more workers. They employed nearly *one-tenth* (1,380,000) of the total number of workers employed in industry and utilised *almost one-third* (32 per cent) of the total steam and electric power employed.[1] As we shall see, money capital and the banks make this superiority of a handful of the largest enterprises still more overwhelming, in the most literal sense of the word, since millions of small, medium, and even some big "masters" are in fact in complete subjection to some hundreds of millionaire financiers.

In another advanced country of modern capitalism, the United States, the growth of the concentration of production is still greater. Here statistics single out industry in the narrow sense of the word and group enterprises according to the value of their annual output. In 1904 large-scale enterprises with an annual output of one million dollars and over numbered 1,900 (out of 216,180, *i.e.*, 0.9 per cent). These employed 1,400,000 workers (out of 5,500,000, *i.e.*, 25.6 per cent) and their combined annual output was valued at $5,600,000,000 (out of $14,800,000,000, *i.e.*, 38 per cent). Five years later, in 1909, the corresponding figures were: large-scale enterprises: 3,060 out of 268,491, *i.e.*, 1.1 per cent; employing: 2,000,000 workers out of 6,600,000, *i.e.*, 30.5 per cent; output: $9,000,000,000 out of $20,700,000,000, *i.e.*, 43.8 per cent.[2]

Almost half the total production of all the enterprises of the country was carried on by a *hundredth part* of those enterprises! These 3,000 giant enterprises embrace 268 branches of industry. From this it can be seen that, at a certain stage of its development, concentration itself, as it were, leads right to monopoly; for a score or so of giant enterprises can easily arrive at an agreement, while on the other hand, the difficulty of competition and the tendency towards monopoly arise from the very dimensions of the enterprises. This transformation of competition into monopoly is one of the most important—if not the most important—phenomena of modern capitalist economy, and we must deal with it in greater detail. But first we must clear up one possible misunderstanding.

[1] *Annalen des Deutschen Reichs* (*Annals of the German Empire*), 1911, pp. 165-169.
[2] *Statistical Abstract of the United States*, 1912, p. 202.

American statistics say: 3,000 giant enterprises in 250 branches of industry, as if there were only a dozen large-scale enterprises for each branch of industry.

But this is not the case. Not in every branch of industry are there large-scale enterprises; and, moreover, a very important feature of capitalism in its highest stage of development is so-called "combined production," that is to say, the grouping in a single enterprise of different branches of industry, which either represent the consecutive stages in the working up of raw materials (for example, the smelting of iron ore into pig iron, the conversion of pig iron into steel, and then, perhaps, the manufacture of steel goods)—or are auxiliary to one another (for example, the utilisation of waste or of by-products, the manufacture of packing materials, etc.).

"Combination," writes Hilferding, "levels out the fluctuations of trade and therefore assures to the combined enterprises a more stable rate of profit. Secondly, combination has the effect of eliminating trading. Thirdly, it has the effect of rendering possible technical improvements, and, consequently, the acquisition of superprofits over and above those obtained by the 'pure' (*i.e.*, *non-combined*) enterprises. Fourthly, it strengthens the position of the combined enterprises compared with that of 'pure' enterprises in the competitive struggle in periods of serious depression, when the fall in prices of raw materials does not keep pace with the fall in prices of manufactured articles." [3]

The German bourgeois economist, Heymann, who has written a book especially on "mixed," that is, combined, enterprises in the German iron industry, says: "Pure enterprises perish, crushed between the high price of raw material and the low price of the finished product." Thus we get the following picture:

"There remain, on the one hand, the great coal companies, producing millions of tons yearly, strongly organized in their coal syndicate, and on the other, the great steel works, closely allied to the coal mines, having their own steel syndicate. These giant enterprises, producing 400,000 tons of steel per annum, with correspondingly extensive coal, ore and blast furnace plants, as well as the manufacturing of finished goods, employing 10,000 workers quartered in company houses, some-

[3] Rudolf Hilferding, *Das Finanzkapital* (*Finance Capital*), Vienna, 1910, p. 239.

times owning their own ports and railroads, are today the standard type of German iron and steel plant. And concentration still continues. Individual enterprises are becoming larger and larger. An ever increasing number of enterprises in one given industry, or in several different industries, join together in giant combines, backed up and controlled by half a dozen Berlin banks. In the German mining industry, the truth of the teachings of Karl Marx on concentration is definitely proved, at any rate in a country like ours where it is protected by tariffs and freight rates. The German mining industry is ripe for expropriation." [4]

Such is the conclusion which a conscientious bourgeois economist, and such are exceptional, had to arrive at. It must be noted that he seems to place Germany in a special category because her industries are protected by high tariffs. But the concentration of industry and the formation of monopolist manufacturers' combines, cartels, syndicates, etc., could only be accelerated by these circumstances. It is extremely important to note that in free-trade England, concentration *also* leads to monopoly, although somewhat later and perhaps in another form. Professor Hermann Levy, in his special work of research entitled *Monopolies, Cartels and Trusts,* based on data on British economic development, writes as follows:

"In Great Britain it is the size of the enterprise and its capacity which harbour a monopolist tendency. This, for one thing, is due to the fact that the great investment of capital per enterprise, once the concentration movement has commenced, gives rise to increasing demands for new capital for the new enterprises and thereby renders their launching more difficult. Moreover (and this seems to us to be the more important point) every new enterprise that wants to keep pace with the gigantic enterprises that have arisen on the basis of the process of concentration would produce such an enormous quantity of surplus goods that it could only dispose of them either by being able to sell them profitably as a result of an enormous increase in demand or by immediately forcing down prices to a level that would be unprofitable both for itself and for the monopoly combines."

[4] Hans Gideon Heymann, *Die gemischten Werke im deutschen Grosseisengewerbe (Combined Plants in the German Big Iron Industry),* Stuttgart, 1904, pp. 256 and 278.

In England, unlike other countries where protective tariffs facilitate the formation of cartels, monopolist alliances of *entrepreneurs,* cartels and trusts arise in the majority of cases only when the number of competing enterprises is reduced to "a couple of dozen or so." "Here the influence of the concentration movement on the formation of large industrial monopolies in a whole sphere of industry stands out with crystal clarity." [5]

Fifty years ago, when Marx was writing *Capital,* free competition appeared to most economists to be a "natural law." Official science tried, by a conspiracy of silence, to kill the works of Marx, which by a theoretical and historical analysis of capitalism showed that free competition gives rise to the concentration of production, which, in turn, at a certain stage of development, leads to monopoly. Today, monopoly has become a fact. The economists are writing mountains of books in which they describe the diverse manifestations of monopoly, and continue to declare in chorus that "Marxism is refuted." But facts are stubborn things, as the English proverb says, and they have to be reckoned with, whether we like it or not. The facts show that differences between capitalist countries, *e.g.,* in the matter of protection or free trade, only give rise to insignificant variations in the form of monopolies or in the moment of their appearance; and that the rise of monopolies, as the result of the concentration of production, is a general and fundamental law of the present stage of development of capitalism.

For Europe, the time when the new capitalism *definitely* superseded the old can be established with fair precision: it was the beginning of the twentieth century. In one of the latest compilations on the history of the "formation of monopolies," we read:

"A few isolated examples of capitalist monopoly could be cited from the period preceding 1860; in these could be discerned the embryo of the forms that are common today; but all this undoubtedly represents pre-history. The real beginning of modern monopoly goes back, at the earliest, to the 'sixties. The first important period of development of monopoly commenced with the international industrial depression of

[5] Hermann Levy, *Monopole, Kartelle und Trusts* (*Monopolies, Cartels and Trusts*), Jena, 1909, pp. 286, 290, 298.

the 'seventies and lasted until the beginning of the 'nineties....If we examine the question on a European scale, we will find that the development of free competition reached its apex in the 'sixties and 'seventies. Then it was that England completed the construction of its old style capitalist organisation. In Germany, this organisation had entered into a fierce struggle with handicraft and domestic industry, and had begun to create for itself its own forms of existence....

"The great revolutionisation commenced with the crash of 1873, or rather, the depression which followed it and which, with hardly discernible interruptions in the early 'eighties, and the unusually violent, but short-lived boom about 1889, marks twenty-two years of European economic history.... During the short boom of 1889-90, the system of cartels was widely resorted to in order to take advantage of the favourable business conditions. An ill-considered policy drove prices still higher than would have been the case otherwise and nearly all these cartels perished ingloriously in the smash. Another five-year period of bad trade and low prices followed, but a new spirit reigned in industry; the depression was no longer regarded as something to be taken for granted: it was regarded as nothing more than a pause before another boom.

"The cartel movement entered its second epoch: instead of being a transitory phenomenon, the cartels became one of the foundations of economic life. They are winning one field after another, primarily, the raw materials industry. At the beginning of the 'nineties the cartel system had already acquired—in the organisation of the coke syndicate on the model of which the coal syndicate was later formed—a cartel technique which could hardly be improved. For the first time the great boom at the close of the nineteenth century and the crisis of 1900-03 occurred entirely—in the mining and iron industries at least—under the *ægis* of the cartels. And while at that time it appeared to be something novel, now the general public takes it for granted that large spheres of economic life have been, as a general rule, systematically removed from the realm of free competition." [6]

Thus, the principal stages in the history of monopolies are the

---

[6] Th. Vogelstein: *Die finanzielle Organisation der kapitalistischen Industrie und die Monopolbildungen (Financial Organisation of Capitalist Industry and the Formation of Monopolies)* in *Grundriss der Sozialökonomik (Outline of Social Economics)*, 1914, *Tüb.*, Sec. VI, pp. 222 *et seq.* See also by the same author: *Organisationsformen des Eisenindustrie und der Textilindustrie in England und Amerika*, Bd. I., Lpz. 1910 (*The Organisational Forms of the Iron and Textile Industries of England and America*, Vol. 1, Leipzig, 1910).

following: 1) 1860-70, the highest stage, the apex of development of free competition; monopoly is in the barely discernible, embryonic stage. 2) After the crisis of 1873, a wide zone of development of cartels; but they are still the exception. They are not yet durable. They are still a transitory phenomenon. 3) The boom at the end of the nineteenth century and the crisis of 1900-03. Cartels become one of the foundations of the whole of economic life. Capitalism has been transformed into imperialism.

Cartels come to an agreement on the conditions of sale, terms of payment, etc. They divide the markets among themselves. They fix the quantity of goods to be produced. They fix prices. They divide the profits among the various enterprises, etc.

The number of cartels in Germany was estimated at about 250 in 1896 and at 385 in 1905, with about 12,000 firms participating.[7] But it is generally recognised that these figures are underestimations. From the statistics of German industry for 1907 we quoted above, it is evident that even 12,000 large enterprises control certainly more than half the steam and electric power used in the country. In the United States, the number of trusts in 1900 was 185, and in 1907, 250.

American statistics divide all industrial enterprises into three categories, according to whether they belong to individuals, to private firms or to corporations. These latter in 1904 comprised 23.6 per cent, and in 1909, 25.9 per cent (*i.e.,* more than one-fourth of the total industrial enterprises in the country). These employed in 1904, 70.6 per cent, and in 1909, 75.6 per cent (*i.e.,* more than three-fourths) of the total wage earners. Their output amounted at these two dates to $10,900,000,000 and to $16,300,000,000, *i.e,* to 73.7 per cent and 79 per cent of the total respectively.

Not infrequently cartels and trusts concentrate in their hands seven or eight tenths of the total output of a given branch of

[7] Dr. Riesser, *Die deutschen Grossbanken und ihre Konzentration im Zusammenhang mit der Entwicklung der Gesamtwirtschaft in Deutschland* (*The German Big Banks and their Concentration in Connection with the Development of the General Economy in Germany*), fourth ed., 1912, p. 149; *cf.* also Robert Liefmann, *Kartelle und Trusts und die Weiterbildung der volkswirtschaftlichen Organisation* (*Cartels and Trusts and the Further Development of Economic Organisation*), second ed., 1910, p. 25.

industry. The Rhine-Westphalian Coal Syndicate, at its foundation in 1893, controlled 86.7 per cent of the total coal output of
the area. In 1910, it controlled 95.4 per cent.[8] The monopoly so
created assures enormous profits, and leads to the formation of
technical productive units of formidable magnitude. The famous
Standard Oil Company in the United States was founded in
1900:[9]

"It has an authorised capital of $150,000,000. It issued $100,000,000
common and $106,000,000 preferred stock. From 1900 to 1907 the fol-
lowing dividends were paid on this stock: 48, 48, 45, 44, 36, 40, 40, 40
per cent, in the respective years, *i.e.*, in all, $367,000,000. From 1882
to 1907, out of a total net profits to the amount of $889,000,000,
$606,000,000 were distributed in dividends, and the rest went to reserve
capital.... In 1907 the various works of the United States Steel Corporation employed no less than 210,180 workers and other employees.
The largest enterprise in the German mining industry, the Gelsen-
kirchen Mining Company (*Gelsenkirchner Bergwerksgesellschaft*) employed in 1908 46,048 persons."[10]

In 1902, the United States Steel Corporation had already produced 9,000,000 tons of steel.[11] Its output constituted in 1901, 66.3
per cent, and in 1908, 56.1 per cent of the total output of steel
in the United States.[12] The output of mineral ore was 43.9 per
cent and 46.3 per cent respectively.

The report of the American Government Commission on Trusts
states:

"The superiority of the trust over competitors is due to the magnitude of its enterprises and their excellent technical equipment. Since its

[8] Dr. Fritz Kestner, *Der Organisationszwang. Eine Untersuchung über die
Kämpfe zwischen Kartellen und Aussenseitern* (*The Compulsion to Organise.
An Investigation of the Struggles between Cartels and Outsiders*), Berlin, 1912,
p. 11.

[9] Holding company was formed in 1899 to replace trust agreement of 1882.—*Ed.*

[10] Robert Liefmann, *Beteiligungs- und Finanzierungsgesellschaften. Eine Studie
über den modernen Kapitalismus und das Effektenwesen* (*Holding and Finance
Companies—A Study in Modern Capitalism and Securities*), first ed., Jena, 1909,
pp. 212 and 218.

[11] Dr. S. Tschierschky, *Kartelle und Trusts*, Göttingen, 1903, p. 13.

[12] Vogelstein, *Organisationsformen* (*Forms of Organisation*), p. 275.

inception, the Tobacco Trust has devoted all its efforts to the substitution of mechanical for manual labour on an extensive scale. With this end in view, it bought up all patents that had anything to do with the manufacture of tobacco and spent enormous sums for this purpose. Many of these patents at first proved to be of no use, and had to be modified by the engineers employed by the trust. At the end of 1906, two subsidiary companies were formed solely to acquire patents. With the same object in view, the trust built its own foundries, machine shops and repair shops. One of these establishments, that in Brooklyn, employs on the average 300 workers; here experiments are carried out on inventions concerning the manufacture of cigarettes, cheroots, snuff, tinfoil for packing, boxes, etc. Here, also, inventions are perfected.[13]

"Other trusts also employ so-called developing engineers whose business it is to devise new methods of production and to test technical improvements. The United States Steel Corporation grants big bonuses to its workers and engineers for all inventions suitable for raising technical efficiency, or for reducing cost of production."[14]

In German large-scale industry, *e.g.*, in the chemical industry, which has developed so enormously during these last few decades, the promotion of technical improvement is organised in the same way. By 1908, the process of concentration production had already given rise to two main groups which, in their way, were in the nature of monopolies. First these groups represented "dual alliances" of two pairs of big factories, each having a capital of from twenty to twenty-one million marks: on the one hand, the former Meister Factory at Höchst and the Cassella Factory at Frankfort-on-Main; and on the other hand, the aniline and soda factory at Ludwigshafen and the former Bayer Factory at Elberfeld. In 1905, one of these groups, and in 1908 the other group, each concluded a separate agreement with yet another big factory. The result was the formation of two "triple alliances," each with a capital of from forty to fifty million marks. And

---

[13] *Report of the Commission of Corporations on the Tobacco Industry*, Washington, 1909, p. 266, cited according to Dr. Paul Tafel, *Die nordamerikanischen Trusts und ihre Wirkungen auf den Fortschritt der Technik* (*North American Trusts and their Effect on Technical Progress*), Stuttgart, 1913, p. 48.

[14] Dr. P. Tafel, *ibid.*, pp. 48-49.

these "alliances" began to come "close" to one another, to reach "an understanding" about prices, etc.[15]

Competition becomes transformed into monopoly. The result is immense progress in the socialisation of production. In particular, the process of technical invention and improvement becomes socialised.

This is no longer the old type of free competition between manufacturers, scattered and out of touch with one another, and producing for an unknown market. Concentration has reached the point at which it is possible to make an approximate estimate of all sources of raw materials (for example, the iron ore deposits) of a country and even, as we shall see, of several countries, or of the whole world. Not only are such estimates made, but these sources are captured by gigantic monopolist combines. An approximate estimate of the capacity of markets is also made, and the combines divide them up amongst themselves by agreement. Skilled labour is monopolised, the best engineers are engaged; the means of transport are captured: railways in America, shipping companies in Europe and America. Capitalism in its imperialist stage arrives at the threshold of the most complete socialisation of production. In spite of themselves, the capitalists are dragged, as it were, into a new social order, a transitional social order from complete free competition to complete socialisation.

Production becomes social, but appropriation remains private. The social means of production remain the private property of a few. The general framework of formally recognised free competition remains, but the yoke of a few monopolists on the rest of the population becomes a hundred times heavier, more burdensome and intolerable.

The German economist, Kestner, has written a book especially on the subject of "the struggle between the cartels and outsiders," *i.e.,* enterprises outside the cartels. He entitled his work *Compulsory Organisation,* although, in order to present capitalism in its true light, he should have given it the title: "Compulsory Sub-

[15] Riesser, *op. cit.,* third ed., pp. 547-48. The newspapers (June 1916) report the formation of a new gigantic trust which is to combine the chemical industry of Germany.

mission to Monopolist Combines." This book is edifying it only
for the list it gives of the modern and civilised methods that
monopolist combines resort to in their striving towards "organisation."

They are as follows: 1) Stopping supplies of raw materials
("one of the most important methods of compelling adherence
to the cartel"); 2) Stopping the supply of labour by means of "alliances" (*i.e.*, of agreements between employers and the trade unions
by which the latter permit their members to work only in cartelised
enterprises); 3) Cutting off deliveries; 4) Closing of trade outlets;
5) Agreements with the buyers, by which the latter undertake
to trade only with the cartels; 6) Systematic price cutting (to
ruin "outside" firms, *i.e.*, those which refuse to submit to the
monopolists. Millions are spent in order to sell goods for a certain
time below their cost price; there were instances when the price
of benzine was thus lowered from 40 to 22 marks, *i.e.*, reduced
almost by half!); 7) Stopping credits; 8) Boycott.

This is no longer competition between small and large-scale
industry, or between technically developed and backward enterprises. We see here the monopolies throttling those which do not
submit to them, to their yoke, to their dictation. This is how this
process is reflected in the mind of a bourgeois economist:

"Even in the purely economic sphere," writes Kestner, "a certain
change is taking place from commercial activity in the old sense of
the word towards organisational-speculative activity. The greatest success no longer goes to the merchant whose technical and commercial
experience enables him best of all to understand the needs of the buyer,
and who is able to discover and effectively awake a latent demand;
it goes to the speculative genius [?!] who knows how to estimate, or
even only to sense in advance the organisational development and the
possibilities of connections between individual enterprises and the
banks." [16]

Translated into ordinary human language this means that the
development of capitalism has arrived at a stage when, although
commodity production still "reigns" and continues to be regarded

[16] Kestner, *op. cit.*, p. 241.—*Ed.*

as the basis of economic life, it has in reality been undermined and the big profits go to the "geniuses" of financial manipulation. At the basis of these swindles and manipulations lies socialised production; but the immense progress of humanity, which achieved this socialisation, goes to benefit the speculators. We shall see later how "on these grounds" reactionary, petty-bourgeois critics of capitalist imperialism dream of going *back* to "free," "peaceful" and "honest" competition.

"The prolonged raising of prices which results from the formation of cartels," says Kestner, "has hitherto been observed only in relation to the most important means of production, particularly coal, iron and potassium, but has never been observed for any length of time in relation to manufactured goods. Similarly, the increase in profits resulting from that has been limited only to the industries which produce means of production. To this observation we must add that the raw materials industry not only has secured advantages from the cartel formation in regard to the growth of income and profitableness, to the detriment of the finished goods industry, but that it has secured also a *dominating position* over the latter, which did not exist under free competition." [17]

The words which we have italicised reveal the essence of the case which the bourgeois economists admit so rarely and so unwillingly, and which the modern defenders of opportunism, led by K. Kautsky, so zealously try to evade and brush aside. Domination, and violence that is associated with it, such are the relationships that are most typical of the "latest phase of capitalist development"; this is what must inevitably result, and has resulted, from the formation of all-powerful economic monopolies.

We will give one more example of the methods employed by the cartels. It is particularly easy for cartels and monopolies to arise when it is possible to capture all the sources of raw materials, or at least, the most important of them. It would be wrong, however, to assume that monopolies do not arise in other industries in which it is impossible to corner the sources of raw materials. The cement industry, for instance, can find its raw materials everywhere. Yet in Germany it is strongly cartelised. The cement

[17] Kestner, *op. cit.*, p. 254.

manufacturers have formed regional syndicates: South German, Rhine-Westphalian, etc. The prices fixed are monopoly prices: 230 to 280 marks a carload (at a cost price of 180 marks!). The enterprises pay a dividend of from 12 per cent to 16 per cent—and let us not forget that the "geniuses" of modern speculation know how to pocket big profits besides those they draw by way of dividends. Now, in order to prevent competition in such a profitable industry, the monopolists resort to sundry stratagems. For example, they spread disquieting rumours about the situation in their industry. Anonymous warnings are published in the newspapers, like the following: "Investors, don't place your capital in the cement industry!" They buy up "outsiders" (those outside the syndicates) and pay them "indemnities" of 60,000, 80,000 and even 150,000 marks.[18] Monopoly everywhere hews a path for itself without scruple as to the means, from "modestly" buying off competitors to the American device of "employing" dynamite against them.

The statement that cartels can abolish crises is a fable spread by bourgeois economists who at all costs desire to place capitalism in a favourable light. On the contrary, when monopoly appears in *certain* branches of industry, it increases and intensifies the anarchy inherent in capitalist production *as a whole*. The disparity between the development of agriculture and that of industry, which is characteristic of capitalism, is increased. The privileged position of the most highly cartelised industry, so-called *heavy* industry, especially coal and iron, causes "a still greater lack of concerted organisation" in other branches of production—as Jeidels, the author of one of the best works on the relationship of the German big banks to industry, puts it.[19]

"The more developed an economic system is," writes Liefmann, one of the most unblushing apologists of capitalism, "the more it resorts to risky enterprises, or enterprises abroad, to those which need a great

18 Ludwig Eschwege, *Zement*, in *Die Bank*, 1909, Vol. I, p. 115 *et seq.*

19 Otto Jeidels, *Das Verhältnis der deutschen Grossbanken zur Industrie, mit besonderer Berücksichtigung der Eisenindustrie* (*The Relationship of the German Big Banks to Industry, with Special Reference to the Iron Industry*), Leipzig, 1905, p. 271.

deal of time to develop, or finally, to those which are only of local importance." [20]

The increased risk is connected in the long run with the prodigious increase of capital, which overflows the brim, as it were, flows abroad, etc. At the same time the extremely rapid rate of technical progress gives rise more and more to disturbances in the co-ordination between the various spheres of national economy, to anarchy and crisis. Liefmann is obliged to admit that:

"In all probability mankind will see further important technical revolutions in the near future which will also affect the organisation of the economic system...." (For example, electricity and aviation.) "As a general rule, in such periods of radical economic change, speculation develops on a large scale." [21]

Crises of every kind—economic crises more frequently, but not only these—in their turn increase very considerably the tendency towards concentration and monopoly. In this connection, the following reflections of Jeidels on the significance of the crisis of 1900, which, as we have already seen, marked the turning point in the history of modern monopoly, are exceedingly instructive.

"Side by side with the giant plants in the basic industries, the crisis of 1900 found many plants organised on lines that today would be considered obsolete, the 'pure' [non-combined] plants, which had arisen on the crest of the industrial boom. The fall in prices and the falling off in demand put these 'pure' enterprises into a precarious position, which did not affect the big combined enterprises at all, or only affected them for a very short time. As a consequence of this the crisis of 1900 resulted in a far greater concentration of industry than former crises, like that of 1873. The latter crisis also produced a sort of selection of the best equipped enterprises, but owing to the level of technical development at that time, this selection could not place the firms which successfully emerged from the crisis in a position of monopoly. Such a durable monopoly exists to a high degree in the gigantic enterprises in the modern iron and steel and electrical industries, and to a lesser degree, in the engineering industry and certain metal, transport and

[20] Robert Liefmann, *Beteiligungs- und Finanzierungsgesellschaften* (*Holding and Finance Companies*), p. 434.

[21] *Ibid.*, pp. 465-6.

other branches in consequence of their complicated technique, their extensive organisation and the magnitude of their capital." [22]

Monopoly! This is the last word in the "latest phase of capitalist development." But we shall only have a very insufficient, incomplete, and poor notion of the real power and the significance of modern monopolies if we do not take into consideration the part played by the banks.

[22] Jeidels, *op. cit.*, p. 108.

CHAPTER II

The Banks and Their New Role

THE principal and primary function of banks is to serve as an intermediary in the making of payments. In doing so they transform inactive money capital into active capital, that is, into capital producing a profit; they collect all kinds of money revenues and place them at the disposal of the capitalist class.

As banking develops and becomes concentrated in a small number of establishments the banks become transformed, and instead of being modest intermediaries they become powerful monopolies having at their command almost the whole of the money capital of all the capitalists and small business men and also a large part of the means of production and of the sources of raw materials of the given country and in a number of countries. The transformation of numerous modest intermediaries into a handful of monopolists represents one of the fundamental processes in the transformation of capitalism into capitalist imperialism. For this reason we must first of all deal with the concentration of banking.

In 1907-08, the combined deposits of the German joint stock banks, each having a capital of more than a million marks, amounted to 7,000,000,000 marks, while in 1912-13, they amounted to 9,800,000,000 marks. Thus, in five years their deposits increased by 40 per cent. Of the 2,800,000,000 increase, 2,750,000,000 was divided amongst 57 banks, each having a capital of more than 10,000,000 marks. The distribution of the deposits between big and small banks was as follows:[1]

PERCENTAGE OF TOTAL DEPOSITS

Year	IN 9 BIG BERLIN BANKS	IN THE OTHER 48 BANKS WITH A CAPITAL OF MORE THAN 10 MILLION MARKS	IN 115 BANKS WITH A CAPITAL OF 1 TO 10 MILLION MARKS	IN THE SMALL BANKS WITH A CAPITAL OF LESS THAN 1 MILLION MARKS
1907-08	47	32.5	16.5	4
1912-13	49	36	12.	3

[1] Alfred Lansburgh, *Fünf Jahre deutsches Bankwesen (Five Years of German Banking)*, in *Die Bank*, No. 8, 1913, S. 728.

The small banks are being pushed aside by the big banks, of which nine concentrate in their hands almost half the total deposits. But we have left out of account many important details, for instance, the transformation of numerous small banks practically into branches of big banks, etc. Of this we shall speak later on.

At the end of 1913, Schulze-Gaevernitz estimated the deposits in the nine big Berlin banks at 5,100,000,000 marks, out of a total of about 10,000,000,000 marks. Taking into account not only the deposits, but the total resources of these banks, this author wrote:

"At the end of 1909, the nine big Berlin banks, *together* with their *affiliated banks* controlled 11,276,000,000 marks...that is, about 83 per cent of the total German bank capital. The Deutsche Bank, *which together with its affiliated banks* controls nearly 3,000,000,000 marks, represents, parallel with the Prussian State Railway Administration, the biggest and also the most decentralised accumulation of capital in the old world." [2]

We have emphasised the reference to the "affiliated" banks because this is one of the most important features of modern capitalist concentration. Large-scale enterprises, especially the banks, not only completely absorb small ones, but also "join" them to themselves, subordinate them, bring them into their "own" group or *concern* (to use the technical term) by having "holdings" in their capital, by purchasing or exchanging shares, by controlling them through a system of credits, etc., etc. Professor Liefmann has written a voluminous "work" of about 500 pages describing modern "holding and finance companies," [3] unfortunately adding "theoretical" reflections of a very poor quality to what is frequently partly digested raw material. To what results this "holding" system leads in regard to concentration is best illustrated in the book written

2 Schulze-Gaevernitz. *Die deutsche Kreditbank, Grundriss der Sozialökonomik (The German Credit Bank* in *Outline of Social Economics*), Sec. V, Part II, *Tübingen*, 1915, pp. 12 and 137.

3 Robert Liefmann, *Beteiligungs- und Finanzierungsgesellschaften. Eine Studie über den modernen Kapitalismus und das Effektenwesen (Holding and Finance Companies—A Study in Modern Capitalism and Securities*), first ed., Jena, 1909, p. 212.

on the big German banks by the banker Riesser. But before examining his data, we will quote an example of the "holding" system.

The Deutsche Bank group is one of the biggest, if not the biggest banking group. In order to trace the main threads which connect all the banks in this group, it is necessary to distinguish between holdings of the first, second and third degree, or what amounts to the same thing, between dependence (of the lesser establishments on the Deutsche Bank) in the first, second and third degree. We then obtain the following picture: [4]

THE DEUTSCHE BANK PARTICIPATES:

	PERMANENTLY	FOR AN INDEFINITE PERIOD	OCCASIONALLY	TOTAL
1st degree	in 17 banks	in 5 banks	in 8 banks	in 30 banks
2nd degree	of which 9 participate in 34 others		of which 5 participate in 14 others	of which 14 participate in 48 others
3rd degree	of which 4 participate in 7 others		of which 2 participate in 2 others	of which 6 participate in 9 others

Included in the eight banks dependent on the Deutsche Bank in the "first degree," "occasionally," there are three foreign banks: one Austrian, the Wiener Bankverein, and two Russian, the Siberian Commercial Bank and the Russian Bank for Foreign Trade. Altogether, the Deutsche Bank group comprises, directly and indirectly, partially and totally, no less than 87 banks; and the capital—its own and others which it controls—is estimated at between two and three billion marks.

It is obvious that a bank which stands at the head of such a group, and which enters into agreement with a half dozen other banks only slightly smaller than itself for the purpose of conducting big and profitable operations like floating state loans, is

[4] A. Lansburgh, *Das Beteiligungssystem im deutschen Bankwesen* (*The Holding System in German Banking*), in *Die Bank*, 1910, I, p. 500 *et seq.*

no longer a mere "intermediary" but a combine of a handful of monopolists.

The rapidity with which the concentration of banking proceeded in Germany at the end of the nineteenth and the beginning of the twentieth centuries is shown by the following data which we quote in an abbreviated form from Riesser:

SIX BIG BERLIN BANKS

Year	BRANCHES IN GERMANY	DEPOSIT BANKS AND EXCHANGE OFFICES	CONSTANT HOLD-INGS IN GERMAN JOINT STOCK BANKS	TOTAL ESTABLISH-MENTS
1895	16	14	1	42
1900	21	40	8	80
1911	104	276	63	450

We see the rapid extension of a close network of canals which cover the whole country, centralising all capital and all revenues, transforming thousands and thousands of scattered economic enterprises into a single national, capitalist, and then into an international, capitalist, economic unit. The "decentralisation" that Schulze-Gaevernitz, as an exponent of modern bourgeois political economy, speaks of in the passage previously quoted, really means the subordination of an increasing number of formerly relatively "independent," or rather, strictly local economic units, to a single centre. In reality it is *centralisation,* the increase in the role, the importance and the power of monopolist giants.

In the older capitalist countries this "banking network" is still more close. In Great Britain (including Ireland) in 1910, there were in all 7,151 branches of banks. Four big banks had more than 400 branches each (from 447 to 689); four had more than 200 branches each, and eleven more than 100 each.

In France, *three* big banks (Crédit Lyonnais, the Comptoir National d'Escompte and the Société Générale) extended their operations and their network of branches in the following manner:[5]

---

[5] Eugen Kaufmann, *Das französische Bankwesen* (*French Banking*), Tübingen, 1911, pp. 356 and 362.

	Number of branches and offices			Capital in million francs	
Year	IN THE PROVINCES	IN PARIS	TOTAL	OWN CAPITAL	BORROWED CAPITAL
1870	47	17	64	200	427
1890	192	66	258	265	1,245
1909	1,033	196	1,229	887	4,363

In order to show the "connections" of a big modern bank, Riesser gives the following figures of the number of letters dispatched and received by the Disconto-Gesellschaft, one of the biggest banks in Germany and in the world, the capital of which amounted to 300,000,000 marks in 1914:

Year	LETTERS RECEIVED	LETTERS DISPATCHED
1852	6,135	6,292
1870	85,800	87,513
1900	533,102	626,043

In 1875, the big Paris bank, the Crédit Lyonnais, had 28,535 accounts. In 1912 it had 633,539.[6]

These simple figures show perhaps better than long explanations how the concentration of capital and the growth of their turnover is radically changing the significance of the banks. Scattered capitalists are transformed into a single collective capitalist. When carrying the current accounts of a few capitalists, the banks, as it were, transact a purely technical and exclusively auxiliary operation. When, however, these operations grow to enormous dimensions we find that a handful of monopolists control all the operations, both commercial and industrial, of the whole of capitalist society. They can, by means of their banking connections, by running current accounts and transacting other financial operations, first *ascertain exactly* the position of the various capitalists, then *control* them, influence them by restricting or enlarging, facilitating or hindering their credits, and finally they can *entirely determine* their fate, determine their income, deprive them of capi-

[6] Jean Lescure, *L'épargne en France* (*Savings in France*), Paris, 1914, p. 52.

tal, or, on the other hand, permit them to increase their capital rapidly and to enormous dimensions, etc.

We have just mentioned the 300,000,000 marks' capital of the Disconto-Gesellschaft of Berlin. The increase of the capital of this bank was one of the incidents in the struggle for hegemony between two of the biggest Berlin banks—the Deutsche Bank and the Disconto.

In 1870, the Deutsche Bank, a new enterprise, had a capital of only 15,000,000 marks, while that of the Disconto was 30,000,000 marks. In 1908, the first had a capital of 200,000,000, while the second had 170,000,000. In 1914, the Deutsche Bank increased its capital to 250,000,000 and the Disconto, by merging with a very important bank, the Schaffhausenscher Bankverein, increased its capital to 300,000,000. And, of course, while this struggle for hegemony goes on the two banks more and more frequently conclude "agreements" of an increasingly durable character with each other. This development of banking compels specialists in the study of banking questions—who regard economic questions from a standpoint which does not in the least exceed the bounds of the most moderate and cautious bourgeois reformism—to arrive at the following conclusions:

The German review, *Die Bank,* commenting on the increase of the capital of the Disconto-Gesellschaft to 300,000,000 marks, writes:

"Other banks will follow this same path and in time the three hundred men, who today govern Germany economically, will gradually be reduced to fifty, twenty-five or still fewer. It cannot be expected that this new move towards concentration will be confined to banking. The close relations that exist between certain banks naturally involve the bringing together of the manufacturing concerns which they favour.... One fine morning we shall wake up in surprise to see nothing but trusts before our eyes, and to find ourselves faced with the necessity of substituting state monopolies for private monopolies. However, we have nothing to reproach ourselves with, except with us having allowed things to follow their own course, slightly accelerated by the manipulation of stocks." [7]

[7] A. Lansburgh, *Die Bank mit den 300 Millionen (The 300 Million Mark Bank),* in *Die Bank,* 1914, I, p. 426.

This is an example of the impotence of bourgeois journalism which differs from bourgeois science only in that the latter is less sincere and strives to obscure essential things, to conceal the wood by trees. To be "surprised" at the results of concentration, to "reproach" the government of capitalist Germany, or capitalist "society" ("us"), to fear that the introduction of stocks and shares might "accelerate" concentration in the same way as the German "cartel specialist" Tschierschky fears the American trusts and "prefers" the German cartels on the grounds that they may not, like the trusts, "accelerate technical and economic progress to an excessive degree"[8]—is not this impotence?

But facts remain facts There are no trusts in Germany; there are "only" cartels—but Germany is *governed* by not more than three hundred magnates of capital, and the number of these is constantly diminishing. At all events, banks in all capitalist countries, no matter what the law in regard to them may be, greatly intensify and accelerate the process of concentration of capital and the formation of monopolies.

The banking system, Marx wrote half a century ago in *Capital,* "presents indeed the form of common bookkeeping and distribution of means of production on a social scale, but only the form."[9] The figures we have quoted on the growth of bank capital, on the increase in the number of the branches and offices of the biggest banks, the increase in the number of their accounts, etc., present a concrete picture of this "common bookkeeping" of the *whole* capitalist class; and not only of the capitalists, for the banks collect, even though temporarily, all kinds of financial revenues of small business men, office clerks, and of a small upper stratum of the working class. It is "common distribution of means of production" that, from the formal point of view, grows out of the development of modern banks, the most important of which, numbering from three to six in France, and from six to eight in Germany, control billions and billions. In point of fact, however, the distribution of means

[8] Tschierschky, *op. cit.,* p. 128.

[9] Karl Marx, *Capital* (Three Volumes), new and revised edition, International Publishers, New York, 1967, Volume III, p. 606.—*Ed.*

of production is by no means "common," but private, *i.e.,* it conforms to the interests of big capital, and primarily, of very big monopoly capital, which operates in conditions in which the masses of the population live in want, in which the whole development of agriculture hopelessly lags behind the development of industry, and within industry itself the "heavy industries" exact tribute from all other branches of industry.

The savings banks and post offices are beginning to compete with the banks in the matter of socialising capitalist economy; they are more "decentralised," *i.e.,* their influence extends to a greater number of localities, to more remote places, to wider sections of the population. An American commission has collected the following data on the comparative growth of deposits in banks and savings banks:[10]

DEPOSITS (*in billions of marks*)

| | ENGLAND | | FRANCE | | GERMANY | | |
Year	BANKS	SAVINGS BANKS	BANKS	SAVINGS BANKS	BANKS	CREDIT SOCIETIES	SAVINGS BANKS
1880	8.4	1.6	?	0.9	0.5	0.4	2.6
1888	12.4	2.0	1.5	2.1	1.1	0.4	4.5
1908	23.2	4.2	3.7	4.2	7.1	2.2	13.9

As they pay interest at the rate of 4 per cent and 4¼ per cent on deposits, the savings banks must seek "profitable" investments for their capital, they must deal in bills, mortgages, etc. The boundaries between the banks and the savings banks "become more and more obliterated." The Chambers of Commerce at Bochum and Erfurt, for example, demand that savings banks be prohibited from engaging in "purely" banking business, such as discounting bills. They demand the limitation of the "banking" operations of the post office.[11] The banking magnates seem to be afraid that state monopoly will steal upon them from an unexpected quarter. It goes without saying, however, that this fear is no more than the expression, as it were, of the rivalry between two department man-

---

[10] *Cf. Statistics of the National Monetary Commission,* quoted in *Die Bank,* 1910, I, p. 1200.

[11] *Die Bank,* 1913, I, 811, 1022; 1914, p. 743.

agers in the same office; for, on the one hand, the billions entrusted
to the savings banks are in the final analysis actually controlled
by *these very same* bank magnates, while, on the other hand, state
monopoly in capitalist society is nothing more than a means of
increasing and guaranteeing the income of millionaires on the
verge of bankruptcy in one branch of industry or another.

The change from the old type of capitalism, in which free competition predominated, to the new capitalism, in which monopoly
reigns, is expressed, among other things, by a decrease in the importance of the Stock Exchange. The German review, *Die Bank,*
wrote:

"For a long time now, the Stock Exchange has ceased to be the
indispensable intermediary of circulation that it was formerly when the
banks were not yet able to place the bulk of new issues with their
clients." [12]

"Every bank is a Stock Exchange, and the bigger the bank, and the
more successful the concentration of banking, the truer does this proverb
become." [13]

"While formerly, in the 'seventies, the Stock Exchange, flushed
with the exuberance of youth" (a "subtle" allusion to the crash of
1873, and to the company promotion scandals), "opened the era
of the industrialisation of Germany, nowadays the banks and
industry are able to 'do it alone.' The domination of our big
banks over the Stock Exchange...is nothing else than the expression of the completely organised German industrial state. If
the domain of the automatically functioning economic laws is thus
restricted, and if the domain consciously regulated by the banks
is considerably increased, the national economic responsibility of
a very small number of guiding heads is infinitely increased," [14]
so wrote Professor Schulze-Gaevernitz, an apologist of German
imperialism, who is regarded as an authority by the imperialists
of all countries, and who tries to gloss over a "detail," *viz.,* that

[12] *Die Bank,* 1914, I, p. 316.
[13] Oskar Stillich, *Geld und Bankwesen* (*Money and Banking*), Berlin, 1907,
p. 169.
[14] Schulze-Gaevernitz, *Die deutsche Kreditbank, Grundriss der Sozialökonomik*
(*German Credit Bank* in *Outline of Social Economics*), Tübingen, 1915. Schulze-
Gaevernitz, *ibid.,* p. 151.

the "conscious regulation" of economic life by the banks consists
in the fleecing of the public by a handful of "completely organised"
monopolists. For the task of a bourgeois professor is not to lay
bare the mechanism of the financial system, or to divulge all the
machinations of the finance monopolists, but, rather, to present
them in a favourable light.

In the same way, Riesser, a still more authoritative economist
and himself a bank man, makes shift with meaningless phrases in
order to explain away undeniable facts. He writes:

"... The Stock Exchange is steadily losing the feature which is absolutely essential for national economy as a whole and for the circulation
of securities in particular—that of being an exact measuring-rod and
an almost automatic regulator of the economic movements which con-
verge on it." [15]

In other words, the old capitalism, the capitalism of free competition, and its indispensable regulator, the Stock Exchange, are passing away. A new capitalism has come to take its place, which
bears obvious features of something transitory, which is a mixture
of free competition and monopoly. The question naturally arises: to
what is this new, "transitory" capitalism leading? But the bourgeois
scholars are afraid to raise this question.

"Thirty years ago, employers, freely competing against one another,
performed nine-tenths of the work connected with their businesses other
than manual labour. At the present time, nine-tenths of this business
'brain work' is performed by *officials*. Banking is in the forefront of
this evolution." [16]

This admission by Schulze-Gaevernitz brings us once again to
the question as to what this new capitalism, capitalism in its imperialist stage, is leading to.

Among the few banks which remain at the head of all capitalist
economy as a result of the process of concentration, there is naturally to be observed an increasingly marked tendency towards
monopolist agreements, towards a *bank trust*. In America, there
are not nine, but *two* big banks, those of the billionaires Rocke-

[15] Riesser, *op. cit.*, fourth ed., p. 629.
[16] *Die Bank*, 1912, p. 435.

feller and Morgan, which control a capital of eleven billion marks.[17] In Germany, the absorption of the Schaffhausenscher Bankverein by the Disconto-Gesellschaft, to which we referred above, was commented on in the following terms by the *Frankfurter Zeitung*, one of the organs of the Stock Exchange interests:

"The concentration movement of the banks is narrowing the circle of establishments from which it is possible to obtain large credits, and is consequently increasing the dependence of big industry upon a small number of banking groups. In view of the internal links between industry and finance, the freedom of movement of manufacturing companies in need of bank capital is restricted. For this reason, big industry is watching the growing trustification of the banks with mixed feelings. Indeed we have repeatedly seen the beginnings of certain agreements between the individual big banking concerns, which aim at limiting competition." [18]

Again, the final word in the development of the banks is monopoly.

The close ties that exist between the banks and industry are the very things that bring out most strikingly the new role of the banks. When a bank discounts a bill for an industrial firm, opens a current account for it, etc., these operations, taken separately, do not in the least diminish the independence of the industrial firm, and the bank plays no other part than that of a modest intermediary. But when such operations are multiplied and become an established practice, when the bank "collects" in its own hands enormous amounts of capital, when the running of a current account for the firm in question enables the bank—and this is what happens—to become better informed of the economic position of the client, then the result is that the industrial capitalist becomes more completely dependent on the bank.

At the same time a very close personal union is established between the banks and the biggest industrial and commercial enterprises the merging of one with another through the acquisition of shares, through the appointment of bank directors to the Supervisory Boards (or Boards of Directors) of industrial and com-

[17] *Die Bank*, 1912, p. 435.
[18] Quoted by Schulze-Gaevernitz, *ibid.*, p. 155.

mercial enterprises, and *vice versa*. The German economist, Jeidels, has compiled very complete data on this form of concentration of capital and of enterprises. Six of the biggest Berlin banks were represented by their directors in 344 industrial companies; and by their board members in 407 other companies. Altogether, they supervised a total of 751 companies. In 289 of these companies they either had two of their representatives on each of the respective Supervisory Boards, or held the posts of chairmen. These industrial and commercial companies are engaged in the most varied branches of industry: in insurance, transport, restaurants, theatres, art industry, etc. On the other hand, there were on the Supervisory Boards of these six banks (in 1910) fifty-one of the biggest manufacturers, among whom were directors of Krupp, of the powerful "Hapag" (Hamburg-American Line), etc. From 1895 to 1910, each of these six banks participated in the share and bond issues of several hundreds of industrial companies (the number ranging from 281 to 419).[19]

The "personal union" between the banks and industry is completed by the "personal union" between both and the state.

"Seats on the Supervisory Board," writes Jeidels, "are freely offered to persons of title, also to ex-civil servants, who are able to do a great deal to facilitate [!!] relations with the authorities....Usually on the Supervisory Board of a big bank there is a member of parliament or a Berlin city councillor."[20]

The building, so to speak, of the great capitalist monopolies is therefore going on full steam ahead in all "natural" and "supernatural" ways. A sort of division of labour amongst some hundreds of kings of finance who reign over modern capitalist society is being systematically developed.

"Simultaneously with this widening of the sphere of activity of certain big industrialists" (sharing in the management of banks, etc.) "and together with the allocation of provincial bank managers to definite industrial regions, there is a growth of specialisation among the managers of the big banks....Generally speaking, this specialisation is only

[19] Jeidels, *op. cit.;* Riesser, *op. cit.—Ed.*
[20] Jeidels, *op. cit.,* pp. 149, 152.—*Ed.*

conceivable when banking is conducted on a large scale, and particularly when it has widespread connections with industry. This division of labour proceeds along two lines: on the one hand, the relations with industry as a whole are entrusted to one manager, as his special function; on the other, each manager assumes the supervision of several isolated enterprises, or enterprises with allied interests, or in the same branch of industry, sitting on their Boards of Directors" (capitalism has reached the stage of organised *control* of individual enterprises). "One specialises in German industry, sometimes even in West German industry alone" (the West is the most industrialised part of Germany). "Others specialise in relations with foreign states and foreign industry, in information about manufacturers, in Stock Exchange questions, etc. Besides, each bank manager is often assigned a special industry or locality, where he has a say as a member of the Board of Directors; one works mainly on the Board of Directors of electric companies, another in the chemical, brewing or sugar beet industry; a third in a few isolated industrial enterprises but at the same time in non-industrial, *i.e.,* insurance companies.... It is certain that, as the extent and diversification of the big banks' operations increase, the division of labour among their directors also spreads, with the object and result of lifting them somewhat out of pure banking and making them better experts, better judges of the general problems of industry and the special problems of each branch of industry, thus making them more capable of action within the respective bank's industrial sphere of influence. This system is supplemented by the banks' endeavours to have elected to their own Board of Directors, or to those of their subsidiary banks, men who are experts in industrial affairs, such as manufacturers, former officials, especially those formerly in the railway service or in mining," etc.[21]

We find the same system, with only slight difference, in French banking. For instance, one of the three biggest French banks, the Crédit Lyonnais, has organised a financial research service (*Service des études financières*), which permanently employs over fifty engineers, statisticians, economists, lawyers, etc., at a cost of six or seven hundred thousand francs annually. The service is in turn divided into eight sections, of which one deals with industrial establishments, another with general statistics, a third with railway and

[21] Jeidels, *op. cit.,* pp. 156-57.

steamship companies, a fourth with securities, a fifth with financial reports, etc.[22]

The result is twofold: on the one hand the merging, to an ever greater extent, or, as N. Bukharin aptly calls it, the coalescence of bank and industrial capital; and on the other hand, a transformation of the banks into institutions of a truly "universal character." On this question we think it necessary to quote the exact terms used by Jeidels, who has best studied the subject:

"An examination of the sum total of industrial relationships reveals the *universal character* of the financial establishments working on behalf of industry. Unlike other kinds of banks and contrary to the requirements often laid down in literature—according to which banks ought to specialise in one kind of business or in one branch of industry in order to maintain a firm footing—the big banks are striving to make their industrial connections as varied and far-reaching as possible, according to locality and branch of business, and are striving to do away with the inequalities in the distribution among localities and branches of business resulting from the historical development of individual banking houses.... One tendency is to make the ties with industry general; another tendency is to make these ties durable and close. In the six big banks both these tendencies are realised, not in full, but to a considerable extent and to an equal degree." [23]

Quite often industrial and commercial circles complain of the "terrorism" of the banks. And it is not surprising that such complaints are heard, for the big banks "command," as will be seen from the following example: on November 19, 1901, one of the big Berlin "D" bank (such is the name given to the four biggest banks whose names begin with the letter D [24]) wrote to the Board of Directors of the German Central Northwest Cement Syndicate in the following terms:

[22] Eugen Kaufmann, *Die Organisation der französischen Depositen-Grossbanken* (*Organisation of the Big French Deposit Banks*), in *Die Bank*, 1909, II, pp. 851 *et seq.*

[23] Jeidels, *op. cit.*, p. 180.

[24] *I.e.*, Deutsche Bank, Disconto-Gesellschaft, Dresdner Bank and Darmstädter Bank.—*Ed.*

"As we learn from the notice you published in the *Reichsanzeiger* of the 18th instant, we must reckon with the possibility that the next general meeting of your company, fixed for the 30th of this month, may decide on measures which are likely to effect changes in your undertakings which are unacceptable to us. We deeply regret that, for these reasons, we are obliged henceforth to withdraw the credit which has been hitherto allowed you....But if the said next general meeting does not decide upon measures which are unacceptable to us and if we receive suitable guarantees on this matter for the future, we shall be quite willing to open negotiations with you on the grant of a new credit." [25]

As a matter of fact, this is small capital's old complaint about being oppressed by big capital, but in this case it was a whole syndicate that fell into the category of "small" capital! The old struggle between big and small capital is being resumed on a new and higher stage of development. It stands to reason that undertakings, financed by big banks handling billions, can accelerate technical progress in a way that cannot possibly be compared with the past. The banks, for example, set up special technical research societies, and only "friendly" industrial enterprises benefit from their work. To this category belong the Electric Railway Research Association and the Central Bureau of Scientific and Technical Research.

The directors of the big banks themselves cannot fail to see that new conditions of national economy are being created. But they are powerless in the face of these phenomena.

"Anyone who has watched, in recent years, the changes of incumbents of directorships and seats on the Supervisory Boards of the big banks, cannot fail to have noticed that power is gradually passing into the hands of men who consider the active intervention of the big banks in the general development of industry to be indispensable and of increasing importance. Between these new men and the old bank directors, disagreements of a business and often of a personal nature are growing on this subject. The question that is in dispute is whether or not the banks, as credit institutions, will suffer from this intervention in industry, whether they are sacrificing tried principles and an assured profit to engage in a field of activity which has nothing in common

[25] Oskar Stillich, *Geld und Bankwesen*, Berlin, 1907, p. 147.

with their role as intermediaries in providing credit, and which is lead-ing the banks into a field where they are more than ever before exposed to the blind forces of trade fluctuations. This is the opinion of many of the older bank directors, while most of the young men consider active intervention in industry to be a necessity as great as that which gave rise, simultaneously with big modern industry, to the big banks and modern industrial banking. The two parties to this discussion are agreed only on one point: and that is, that as yet there are neither firm principles nor a concrete aim in the new activities of the big banks." [26]

The old capitalism has had its day. The new capitalism repre-sents a transition towards something. It is hopeless, of course, to seek for "firm principles and a concrete aim" for the purpose of "reconciling" monopoly with free competition. The admission of the practical men has quite a different ring from the official praises of the charms of "organised" capitalism sung by its apologists, Schulze-Gaevernitz, Liefmann and similar "theoreticians."

At precisely what period were the "new activities" of the big banks finally established? Jeidels gives us a fairly exact answer to this important question:

"The ties between the banks and industrial enterprises, with their new content, their new forms and their new organs, namely, the big banks which are organised on both a centralised and a decentralised basis, were scarcely a characteristic economic phenomenon before the 'nineties; in one sense, indeed, this initial date may be advanced to the year 1897, when the important 'mergers' took place and when, for the first time, the new form of decentralised organisation was introduced to suit the industrial policy of the banks. This starting point could perhaps be placed at an even later date, for it was the crisis [of 1900] that enormously accelerated and intensified the process of concentra-tion of industry and banking, consolidated that process, for the first time transformed the connection with industry into the monopoly of the big banks, and made this connection much closer and more active." [27]

Thus, the beginning of the twentieth century marks the turning point from the old capitalism to the new, from the domination of capital in general to the domination of finance capital.

[26] Jeidels, *op. cit.*, pp. 183-84.
[27] *Ibid.*, p. 181.

CHAPTER III

Finance Capital and Financial Oligarchy

"A steadily increasing proportion of capital in industry," Hilferding writes, "does not belong to the industrialists who employ it. They obtain the use of it only through the medium of the banks, which, in relation to them, represent the owners of the capital. On the other hand, the bank is forced to keep an increasing share of its funds engaged in industry. Thus, to an increasing degree the bank is being transformed into an industrial capitalist. This bank capital, *i.e.,* capital in money form which is thus really transformed into industrial capital, I call 'finance capital.'...Finance capital is capital controlled by banks and employed by industrialists."[1]

This definition is incomplete in so far as it is silent on one extremely important fact: the increase of concentration of production and of capital to such an extent that it leads, and has led, to monopoly. But throughout the whole of his work, and particularly in the two chapters which precede the one from which this definition is taken, Hilferding stresses the part played by *capitalist monopolies.*

The concentration of production; the monopoly arising therefrom; the merging or coalescence of banking with industry—this is the history of the rise of finance capital and what gives the term "finance capital" its content.

We now have to describe how, under the general conditions of commodity production and private property, the "domination" of capitalist monopolies inevitably becomes the domination of a financial oligarchy. It should be noted that the representatives of German bourgeois science—and not only of German science—like Riesser, Schulze-Gaevernitz, Liefmann and others are all apologists of imperialism and of finance capital. Instead of revealing the "mechanics" of the formation of an oligarchy, its methods, its revenues "innocent and sinful," its connections with parliaments, etc., they

[1] R. Hilferding, *Das Finanzkapital,* 1912, p. 283.

47

conceal, obscure and embellish them. They evade these "vexed questions" by a few vague and pompous phrases: appeals to the "sense of responsibility" of bank directors, praising "the sense of duty" of Prussian officials; by giving serious study to petty details, to ridiculous bills of parliament—for the "supervision" and "regulation" of monopolies; by playing with theories, like, for example, the following "scientific" definition, arrived at by Professor Liefmann: *"Commerce is an occupation having for its object: collecting goods, storing them and making them available."* (The Professor's boldface italics.) From this it would follow that commerce existed in the time of primitive man, who knew nothing about exchange, and that it will exist under socialism!

But the monstrous facts concerning the monstrous rule of the financial oligarchy are so striking that in all capitalist countries, in America, France and Germany, a whole literature has sprung up, written from the *bourgeois* point of view, but which, nevertheless, gives a fairly accurate picture and criticism—petty-bourgeois, naturally—of this oligarchy.

The "holding system," to which we have already briefly referred above, should be placed at the corner-stone. The German economist, Heymann, probably the first to call attention to this matter, describes it in this way:

"The head of the concern controls the parent company; the latter reigns over the subsidiary companies which in their turn control still other subsidiaries. Thus, it is possible with a comparatively small capital to dominate immense spheres of production. As a matter of fact, if holding 50 per cent of the capital is always sufficient to control a company, the head of the concern needs only one million to control eight millions in the second subsidiaries. And if this "interlocking" is extended, it is possible with one million to control sixteen, thirty-two or more millions." [2]

Experience shows that it is sufficient to own 40 per cent of the shares of a company in order to direct its affairs, [3] since a certain number of small, scattered shareholders find it impossible, in prac-

[2] Heymann, *Die gemischten Werke im deutschen Grosseisengewerbe*, Stuttgart 1904, pp. 268-69.
[3] R. Liefmann, *Beteiligungsgesellschaften*, p. 258.

tice, to attend general meetings, etc. The "democratisation" of the ownership of shares, from which the bourgeois sophists and opportunist "would-be" Social-Democrats expect (or declare that they expect) the "democratisation of capital," the strengthening of the role and significance of small-scale production, etc., is, in fact, one of the ways of increasing the power of financial oligarchy. Incidentally, this is why, in the more advanced, or in the older and more "experienced" capitalist countries, the law allows the issue of shares of very small denomination. In Germany, it is not permitted by the law to issue shares of less value than one thousand marks, and the magnates of German finance look with an envious eye at England, where the issue of one-pound shares is permitted. Siemens, one of the biggest industrialists and "financial kings" in Germany, told the Reichstag on June 7, 1900, that "the one-pound share is the basis of British imperialism." [4] This merchant has a much deeper and more "Marxian" understanding of imperialism than a certain disreputable writer, generally held to be one of the founders of Russian Marxism, who believes that imperialism is a bad habit of a certain nation....

But the "holding system" not only serves to increase enormously the power of the monopolists; it also enables them to resort with impunity to all sorts of shady tricks to cheat the public, for the directors of the parent company are not legally responsible for the subsidiary companies, which are supposed to be "independent," and *through the medium* of which they can "pull off" *anything*. Here is an example taken from the German review, *Die Bank*, for May 1914:

"The Spring Steel Company of Kassel was regarded some years ago as being one of the most profitable enterprises in Germany. Through bad management its dividends fell within the space of a few years from 15 per cent to nil. It appears that the Board, without consulting the shareholders, had loaned *six million marks* to one of the subsidiary companies, the Hassia, Ltd., which had a nominal capital of only some hundreds of thousands of marks. This commitment, amounting to nearly treble the capital of the parent company, was never mentioned

[4] Schulze-Gaevernitz in *"Grdr. d. S.-Oek.,"* V, 2, p. 110.

in its balance sheets. This omission was quite legal, and could be kept up for two whole years because it did not violate any provision of company law. The chairman of the Supervisory Board, who as the responsible head had signed the false balance sheets, was, and still is, the president of the Kassel Chamber of Commerce. The shareholders only heard of the loan to the Hassia, Ltd., long afterwards, when it had long been proved to have been a mistake" (this word the writer should have put in quotation marks), "and when Spring Steel shares had dropped nearly 100 points, because those in the know had got rid of them....

"*This typical example of balance-sheet jugglery, quite common in joint stock companies,* explains why their Boards of Directors are more willing to undertake risky transactions than individual dealers. Modern methods of drawing up balance sheets not only make it possible to conceal doubtful undertakings from the average shareholder, but also allow the people most concerned to escape the consequence of unsuccessful speculation by selling their shares in time while the individual dealer risks his own skin in everything he does.

"The balance sheets of many joint stock companies put us in mind of the palimpsests of the Middle Ages from which the visible inscription had first to be erased in order to discover beneath it another inscription giving the real meaning of the document." (Palimpsests are parchment documents from which the original inscription has been obliterated and another inscription imposed.)

"The simplest and, therefore, most common procedure for making balance sheets indecipherable is to divide a single business into several parts by setting up subsidiary companies—or by annexing such. The advantages of this system for various objects—legal and illegal—are so evident that it is now quite unusual to find an important company in which it is not actually in use."[5]

As an example of an important monopolist company widely employing this system, the author quotes the famous General Electric Company (Allgemeine Elektrizitäts Gesellschaft—A.E.G.) to which we shall refer below. In 1912, it was calculated that this company held shares in from *175 to 200* other companies, controlling them,

    [5] Ludwig Eschwege, *Tochtergesellschaften* (*Subsidiary Companies*), in *Die Bank*, 1914, I, pp. 544-46.

of course, and thus having control of a total capital of *1,500,000,000 marks!* [6]

All rules of control, the publication of balance sheets, the drawing up of balance sheets according to a definite form, the public auditing of accounts, etc., the things about which well-intentioned professors and officials—that is, those imbued with the good intention of defending and embellishing capitalism—discourse to the public, are of no avail. For private property is sacred, and no one can be prohibited from buying, selling, exchanging or mortgaging shares, etc.

The extent to which this "holding system" has developed in the big Russian banks may be judged by the figures given by E. Agahd, who was for fifteen years an official of the Russo-Chinese Bank and who, in May 1914, published a book, not altogether correctly entitled *Big Banks and the World Market*.[7] The author divides the big Russian banks into two main categories: a) banks that come under a "holding system," and b) "independent" banks—"independence," however, being arbitrarily taken to mean independence of *foreign* banks. The author divides the first group into three sub-groups: 1) German participation, 2) British participation, and 3) French participation, having in view the "participation" and domination of the big foreign banks of the particular country mentioned. The author divides the capital of the banks into "productively" invested capital (in industrial and commercial undertakings), and "speculatively" invested capital (in Stock Exchange and financial operations), assuming, from his petty-bourgeois reformist point of view, that it is possible, under capitalism, to separate the first form of investment from the second and to abolish the second form.

Here are the figures he supplies:

[6] Kurt Heinig, *Der Weg des Elektrotrusts (The Path of the Electric Trust)*, in *Die Neue Zeit*, 1911-1912, Vol. II, p. 484.

[7] E. Agahd, *Grossbanken und Weltmarkt. Die wirtschaftliche und politische Bedeutung der Grossbanken im Weltmark unter Berücksichtigung ihres Einflusses auf Russlands Volkswirtschaft und die deutsch-russischen Beziehungen.* Berl. ("Big Banks and the World Market. The economic and political significance of the big banks on the world market, with reference to their influence on Russia's national economy and German-Russian relations." Berlin, 1914, pp. 11-17.)

BANK ASSETS

(According to reports for October-November, 1913, in millions of rubles)

GROUPS OF RUSSIAN BANKS	CAPITAL INVESTED		
	PRODUCTIVE	SPECULATIVE	TOTAL
A. 1) Four banks: Siberian Commercial Bank, Russian Bank, International Bank, and Discount Bank	413.7	859.1	1,272.8
2) Two banks: Commercial and Industrial and Russo-British	239.3	169.1	408.4
3) Five banks: Russian-Asiatic, St. Petersburg Private, Azov-Don, Union Moscow, Russo-French Commercial	711.8	661.2	1,373.0
Total: (11 banks)	1,364.8	1,689.4	3,054.2
B. Eight banks: Moscow Merchants, Volga-Kama, Junker and Co., St. Petersburg Commercial (formerly Wawelberg), Bank of Moscow (formerly Riabushinsky), Moscow Discount, Moscow Commercial, Private Bank of Moscow	504.2	391.1	895.3
Total: (19 banks)	1,869.0	2,080.5	3,949.5

According to these figures, of the approximately four billion rubles making up the "working" capital of the big banks, *more than three-fourths,* more than three billion, belonged to banks which in reality were only "subsidiary companies" of foreign banks, and chiefly of the Paris banks (the famous trio: Union Parisien, Paris et Pays-Bas and Société Générale), and of the Berlin banks (particularly the Deutsche Bank and Disconto-Gesellschaft). Two of the most important Russian banks, the Russian Bank for Foreign Trade and the St. Petersburg International Commercial, between 1906 and 1912 increased their capital from 44,000,000 to 98,000,000 rubles, and their reserve from 15,000,000 to 39,000,000 "employing three-fourths German capital." The first belongs to the Deutsche Bank group and the second to the Disconto-Gesellschaft. The worthy Agahd is indignant at the fact that the majority of the shares are held by the Berlin banks, and that, therefore, the Russian shareholders are powerless. Naturally, the country which exports capital skims the cream: for example, the Deutsche Bank, while introducing the shares of the Siberian Commercial Bank on the Berlin market, kept them in its portfolio for a whole year, and then sold them at the rate of 193 for 100, that is, at nearly twice their nominal value, "earning" a profit of nearly 6,000,000 rubles, which Hilferding calls "promoters' profits."

Our author puts the total "resources" of the principal St. Petersburg banks at 8,235,000,000 rubles, about 8¼ billions and the "holdings," or rather, the extent to which foreign banks dominated them, he estimates as follows: French banks, 55 per cent; English, 10 per cent; German, 35 per cent. The author calculates that of the total of 8,235,000,000 rubles of functioning capital, 3,687,000,000 rubles, or over 40 per cent, fall to the share of the syndicates, Produgol and Prodamet [8]—and the syndicates in the oil, metallurgical and cement industries. Thus, the merging of bank and industrial capital has also made great strides in Russia owing to the formation of capitalist monpolies.

Finance capital, concentrated in a few hands and exercising a virtual monopoly, exacts enormous and ever-increasing profits from the floating of companies, issue of stock, state loans, etc., tightens the grip of financial oligarchies and levies tribute upon the whole of society for the benefit of monopolists. Here is an example, taken from a multitude of others, of the methods of "business" of the American trusts, quoted by Hilferding: in 1887, Havemeyer founded the Sugar Trust by amalgamating fifteen small firms, whose total capital amounted to $6,500,000. Suitably "watered," as the Americans say, the capital of the trust was increased to $50,000,000. This "over-capitalisation" anticipated the monopoly profits, in the same way as the United States Steel Corporation anticipated its profits by buying up as many iron fields as possible. In fact, the Sugar Trust set up monopoly prices on the market, which secured it such profits that it could pay 10 per

[8] Abbreviated names of the syndicates, "Russian Society for Trade in the Mineral Fuels of the Donetz Basin," and "Society for the Sale of the Products of Russian Metallurgical Works," organized in 1906 and 1901 respectively.—*Ed.*

cent dividend on capital "watered" *sevenfold, or about 70 per cent on the capital actually invested at the time of the creation of the trust!* In 1909, the capital of the Sugar Trust was increased to $90,000,000. In twenty-two years, it had increased its capital more than tenfold.

In France the role of the "financial oligarchy" (*Against the Financial Oligarchy in France,* the title of the well-known book by Lysis, the fifth edition of which was published in 1908) assumed a form that was only slightly different. Four of the most powerful banks enjoy, not a relative, but an "absolute monopoly" in the issue of bonds. In reality, this is a "trust of the big banks." And their monopoly ensures the monopolist profits from bond issues. Usually a country borrowing from France does not get more than 90 per cent of the total of the loan, the remaining 10 per cent goes to the banks and other middlemen. The profit made by the banks out of the Russo-Chinese loans of 400,000,000 francs amounted to 8 per cent; out of the Russian (1904) loan of 800,000,000 francs the profit amounted to 10 per cent; and out of the Moroccan (1904) loan of 62,500,000 francs, to 18.75 per cent. Capitalism, which began its development with petty usury capital, ends its development with gigantic usury capital. "The French," says Lysis, "are the usurers of Europe." All the conditions of economic life are being profoundly modified by this transformation of capitalism. With a stationary population, and stagnant industry, commerce and shipping, the "country" can grow rich by usury. "Fifty persons, representing a capital of 8,000,000 francs, can control 2,000,000,000 francs deposited in four banks." The "holding system," with which we are already familiar, leads to the same result. One of the biggest banks, the Société Générale, for instance, issues 64,000 bonds for one of its subsidiary companies, the Egyptian Sugar Refineries. The bonds are issued at 150 per cent, *i.e.,* the bank gaining 50 centimes on the franc. The dividends of the new company are then found to be fictitious. The "public" lost from 90 to 100 million francs. One of the directors of the Société Générale was a member of the board of directors of the Egyptian Sugar Refineries. Hence it is not surprising that the author is driven to the conclusion that "the French Republic is a financial monarchy"; "it is the complete domination of the financial oligarchy; the latter controls the press and the government."[9]

The extraordinarily high rate of profit obtained from the issue of securities, which is one of the principal functions of finance capital, plays a large part in the development and consolidation of the financial oligarchy.

"There is not within the country a single business of this type that brings in profits even approximately equal to those obtained from the flotation of foreign loans,"[10] says the German magazine, *Die Bank*.

"No banking operation brings in profits comparable with those obtained from the issue of securities!"[11]

According to the *German Economist*, the average annual profits made on the issue of industrial securities were as follows:

	PER CENT		PER CENT
1895	38.6	1898	67.7
1896	36.1	1899	66.9
1897	66.7	1900	55.2

"In the ten years from 1891 to 1900, *more than a billion* marks of profits were 'earned' by issuing German industrial securities."[12]

While, during periods of industrial boom, the profits of finance capital are disproportionately large, during periods of depression, small and unsound businesses go out of existence, while the big banks take "holdings" in their shares, which are bought up cheaply or in profitable schemes for their "reconstruction" and "reorganisation." In the "reconstruction" of undertakings which have been running at a loss,

"the share capital is written down, that is, profits are distributed on a smaller capital and subsequently are calculated on this smaller basis. If the income has fallen to zero, new capital is called in, which, com-

[9] Lysis, *Contre l'oligarchie financière en France* (*Against the Financial Oligarchy in France*) fifth ed., Paris, 1908, pp. 11, 12, 26, 39, 40, 47-48.

[10] *Die Bank*, 1913, II, p. 630.

[11] Stillich, *op. cit.*, p. 143.—*Ed.*

[12] Stillich, *ibid.*; also Werner Sombart, *Die deutsche Volkswirtschaft im 19. Jahrhundert* (*German National Economy in the Nineteenth Century*), second ed., Berlin, 1909, p. 526, Appendix.

bined with the old and less remunerative capital, will bring in an adequate return."

"Incidentally," adds Hilferding, "these reorganisations and reconstructions have a twofold significance for the banks: first, as profitable transactions; and secondly, as opportunities for securing control of the companies in difficulties."[13]

Here is an instance. The Union Mining Company of Dortmund, founded in 1872, with a share capital of nearly 40,000,000 marks, saw the market price of shares rise to 170 after it had paid a 12 per cent dividend in its first year. Finance capital skimmed the cream and earned a "trifle" of something like 28,000,000 marks. The principal sponsor of this company was that very big German Disconto-Gesellschaft which so successfully attained a capital of 300,000,000 marks. Later, the dividends of the Union declined to nil: the shareholders had to consent to a "writing down" of capital, that is, to losing some of it in order not to lose it all. By a series of "reconstructions," more than 73,000,000 marks were written off the books of the Union in the course of thirty years.

"At the present time, the original shareholders of this company possess only 5 per cent of the nominal value of their shares."[14]

But the bank "made a profit" out of every "reconstruction."

Speculation in land situated in the suburbs of rapidly growing towns is a particularly profitable operation for finance capital. The monopoly of the banks merges here with the monopoly of ground rent and with monopoly in the means of communication, since the increase in the value of the land and the possibility of selling it profitably in allotments, etc., is mainly dependent on good means of communication with the centre of the town; and these means of communication are in the hands of large companies which are connected by means of the holding system and by the distribution of positions on the directorates, with the interested banks. As a result we get what the German writer, L. Eschwege, a contributor to *Die Bank,* who has made a special study of real estate business and mortgages, etc., calls the formation of a "bog." Frantic specu-

[13] Hilferding, *op. cit.,* pp. 142-143.
[14] Stillich, *op. cit.,* p. 138, and Liefmann, p. 51.

lation in suburban building lots: collapse of building enterprises (like that of the Berlin firm of Boswau and Knauer, which grabbed 100,000,000 marks with the help of the "sound and solid" Deutsche Bank—the latter acting, of course, discreetly behind the scenes through the holding system and getting out of it by losing "only" 12,000,000 marks), then the ruin of small proprietors and of workers who get nothing from the fraudulent building firms, underhand agreements with the "honest" Berlin police and the Berlin administration for the purpose of getting control of the issue of building sites, tenders, building licenses, etc.[15]

"American ethics," which the European professors and well-meaning bourgeois so hypocritically deplore, have, in the age of finance capital, become the ethics of literally every large city, no matter what country it is in.

At the beginning of 1914, there was talk in Berlin of the proposed formation of a "transport trust," i. e., of establishing "community of interests" between the three Berlin passenger transport undertakings: the Metropolitan electric railway, the tramway company and the omnibus company.

"We know," wrote Die Bank, "that this plan has been contemplated since it became known that the majority of the shares in the bus company has been acquired by the other two transport companies.... We may believe those who are pursuing this aim when they say that by uniting the transport services, they will secure economies part of which will in time benefit the public. But the question is complicated by the fact that behind the transport trust that is being formed are the banks, which, if they desire, can subordinate the means of transportation, which they have monopolised, to the interests of their real estate business. To be convinced of the reasonableness of such a conjecture, we need only recall that at the very formation of the Elevated Railway Company the traffic interests became interlocked with the real estate interests of the big bank which financed it, and this interlocking even created the prerequisites for the formation of the transport enterprise. Its eastern line, in fact, was to run through land which, when it became certain the line was to be laid down, this bank sold to a real estate

---

[15] Ludwig Eschwege, Der Sumpf (The Bog), in Die Bank, 1913, II, p. 952, et seq.; ibid., 1912, I, p. 223 et seq.

firm at an enormous profit for itself and for several partners in the transactions." [16]

A monopoly, once it is formed and controls thousands of millions, inevitably penetrates into *every* sphere of public life, regardless of the form of government and all other "details." In the economic literature of Germany one usually comes across the servile praise of the integrity of the Prussian bureaucracy, and allusions to the French Panama scandal and to political corruption in America. But the fact is that *even* the bourgeois literature devoted to German banking matters constantly has to go far beyond the field of purely banking operations and to speak, for instance, of "the attraction of the banks" in reference to the increasing frequency with which public officials take employment with the banks.

"How about the integrity of a state official who in his inmost heart is aspiring to a soft job in the Behrenstrasse?" [17] (the street in Berlin in which the head office of the Deutsche Bank is situated).

In 1909, the publisher of *Die Bank*, Alfred Lansburgh, wrote an article entitled "The Economic Significance of Byzantinism," in which he incidentally referred to Wilhelm II's tour of Palestine, and to "the immediate result of this journey," the construction of the Bagdad railway, that fatal "standard product of German enterprise, which is more responsible for the 'encirclement' than all our political blunders put together." [18] (By encirclement is meant the policy of Edward VII to isolate Germany by surrounding her with an imperialist anti-German alliance.) In 1912, another contributor to this magazine, Eschwege, to whom we have already referred, wrote an article entitled "Plutocracy and Bureaucracy," in which he exposes the case of a German official named Volker, who was a zealous member of the Cartel Committee and who, some time later, obtained a lucrative post in the biggest cartel, *i.e.*, the Steel Syndicate. [19] Similar cases, by no means casual, forced

[16] *Verkehrstrust* (*Transport Trust*), in *Die Bank*, 1914, I, pp. 89-90.
[17] *Der Zug zur Bank* (*The Attraction of the Banks*), in *Die Bank*, 1909, I, p. 79.
[18] *Ibid.*, p. 307.
[19] *Die Bank*, 1912, II, p. 825.—*Ed.*

this bourgeois author to admit that "the economic liberty guaranteed by the German Constitution has become in many departments of economic life, a meaningless phrase" and that under the existing rule of the plutocracy, "even the widest political liberty cannot save us from being converted into a nation of unfree people."[20]

As for Russia, we will content ourselves by quoting one example. Some years ago, all the newspapers announced that Davidov, the director of the Credit Department of the Treasury, had resigned his post to take employment with a certain big bank at a salary which, according to the contract, was to amount to over one million rubles in the course of several years. The function of the Credit Department is to "co-ordinate the activities of all the credit institutions of the country"; it also grants subsidies to banks in St. Petersburg and Moscow amounting to between 800 and 1,000 million rubles.[21]

It is characteristic of capitalism in general that the ownership of capital is separated from the application of capital to production, that money capital is separated from industrial or productive capital, and that the rentier, who lives entirely on income obtained from money capital, is separated from the entrepreneur and from all who are directly concerned in the management of capital. Imperialism, or the domination of finance capital, is that highest stage of capitalism in which this separation reaches vast proportions. The supremacy of finance capital over all other forms of capital means the predominance of the rentier and of the financial oligarchy; it means the crystallisation of a small number of financially "powerful" states from among all the rest. The extent to which this process is going on may be judged from the statistics on emissions, *i.e.*, the issue of all kinds of securities.

In the Bulletin of the International Statistical Institute, A. Neymarck[22] has published very comprehensive and complete compara-

[20] *Ibid.*, 1913, II, p. 962.

[21] E. Agahd, *op. cit.*, p. 202.

[22] A. Neymarck, *Bulletin de l'institut international de statistique* (*Bulletin of the International Statistical Institute*), Vol. XIX, Book II, The Hague, 1912. Data concerning small states, second column, are approximately calculated by adding 20 per cent to the 1902 figures.

tive figures covering the issue of securities all over the world, which have been repeatedly quoted in economic literature. The following are the totals he gives for four decades:

TOTAL ISSUES IN BILLIONS OF FRANCS (*Decades*)

1871-1880	76.1
1881-1890	64.5
1891-1900	100.4
1901-1910	197.8

In the 1870's, the total amount of issues for the whole world was high, owing particularly to the loans floated in connection with the Franco-Prussian War, and the company-promoting boom which set in in Germany after the war. In general, the increase is not very rapid during the three last decades of the nineteenth century, and only in the first ten years of the twentieth century is an enormous increase observed of almost 100 per cent. Thus the beginning of the twentieth century marks the turning point, not only in regard to the growth of monopolies (cartels, syndicates, trusts), of which we have already spoken, but also in regard to the development of finance capital.

Neymarck estimates the total amount of issued securities current in the world in 1910 at about 815,000,000,000 francs. Deducting from this amounts which might have been duplicated, he reduces the total to 575-600,000,000,000, which is distributed among the various countries as follows (we will take 600,000,000,000):

FINANCIAL SECURITIES CURRENT IN 1910

(*In billions of francs*)

Great Britain	142 ⎤	Japan	12
United States	132 ⎟	Holland	12.5
France	110 ⎬ 479	Belgium	7.5
Germany	95 ⎦	Spain	7.5
Russia	31	Switzerland	6.25
Austria-Hungary	24	Denmark	3.75
Italy	14	Sweden, Norway, Rumania, etc.	2.5
		Total	600.00

From these figures we at once see standing out in sharp relief four of the richest capitalist countries, each of which controls securities to amounts ranging from 100 to 150 billion francs. Two of these countries, England and France, are the oldest capitalist countries, and, as we shall see, possess the most colonies; the other two, the United States and Germany, are in the front rank as regards rapidity of development and the degree of extension of capitalist monopolies in industry. Together, these four countries own 479,000,000,000 francs, that is, nearly 80 per cent of the world's finance capital. Thus, in one way or another, nearly the whole world is more or less the debtor to and tributary of these four international banker countries, the four "pillars" of world finance capital.

It is particularly important to examine the part which export of capital plays in creating the international network of dependence and ties of finance capital.

CHAPTER IV

The Export of Capital

UNDER the old capitalism, when free competition prevailed, the export of *goods* was the most typical feature. Under modern capitalism, when monopolies prevail, the export of *capital* has become the typical feature.

Capitalism is commodity production at the highest stage of development, when labour power itself becomes a commodity. The growth of internal exchange, and particularly of international exchange, is the characteristic distinguishing feature of capitalism. The uneven and spasmodic character of the development of individual enterprises, of individual branches of industry and individual countries, is inevitable under the capitalist system. England became a capitalist country before any other, and in the middle of the nineteenth century, having adopted free trade, claimed to be the "workshop of the world," the great purveyor of manufactured goods to all countries, which in exchange were to keep her supplied with raw materials. But in the last quarter of the nineteenth century, *this* monopoly was already undermined. Other countries, protecting themselves by tariff walls, had developed into independent capitalist states. On the threshold of the twentieth century, we see a new type of monopoly coming into existence. Firstly, there are monopolist capitalist combines in all advanced capitalist countries; secondly, a few rich countries, in which the accumulation of capital reaches gigantic proportions, occupy a monopolist position. An enormous "superabundance of capital" has accumulated in the advanced countries.

It goes without saying that if capitalism could develop agriculture, which today lags far behind industry everywhere, if it could raise the standard of living of the masses, who are everywhere still poverty-stricken and underfed, in spite of the amazing advance in technical knowledge, there could be no talk of a superabundance of capital. This "argument" the petty-bourgeois critics of capitalism advance on every occasion. But if capitalism did these things it would not be capitalism; for uneven development and wretched conditions of the masses are fundamental and inevitable conditions and premises of this mode of production. As long as capitalism remains what it is, surplus capital will never be utilised for the purpose of raising the standard of living of the masses in a given country, for this would mean a decline in profits for the capitalists; it will be used for the purpose of increasing those profits by exporting capital abroad to the backward countries. In these backward countries profits are usually high, for capital is scarce, the price of land is relatively low, wages are low, raw materials are cheap. The possibility of exporting capital is created by the fact that numerous backward countries have been drawn into international capitalist intercourse; main railways have either been built or are being built there; the elementary conditions for industrial development have been created, etc. The necessity for exporting capital arises from the fact that in a few countries capitalism has become "over-ripe" and (owing to the backward state of agriculture and the impoverished state of the masses) capital cannot find "profitable" investment.

Here are approximate figures showing the amount of capital invested abroad by the three principal countries:[1]

CAPITAL INVESTED ABROAD
(In billions of francs)

Year	GREAT BRITAIN	FRANCE	GERMANY
1862	3.6	—	—
1872	15.0	10 (1869)	—
1882	22.0	15 (1880)	?
1893	42.0	20 (1890)	?
1902	62.0	27-37	12.5
1914	75-100	60	44.0

[1] Hobson, *Imperialism*, London, 1902, p. 58; Riesser, *op. cit.*, pp. 395 and 404; P. Arndt in *Weltwirtschaftliches Archiv* (*World Economic Archive*), Vol. VII, 1916, p. 35; Neymarck in *Bulletin de l'institut international de statistique;* Hilferding, *Finanzkapital*, p. 437; Lloyd George, Speech in the House of Commons, May 4, 1915, reported in *Daily Telegraph*, May 5, 1915; B. Harms, *Probleme der Welt-*

This table shows that the export of capital reached formidable dimensions only in the beginning of the twentieth century. Before the war the capital invested abroad by the three principal countries amounted to between 175,000,000,000 and 200,000,000,000 francs. At the modest rate of 5 per cent, this sum should have brought in from 8 to 10 billions a year. This provided a solid basis for imperialist oppression and the exploitation of most of the countries and nations of the world; a solid basis for the capitalist parasitism of a handful of wealthy states!

How is this capital invested abroad distributed among the various countries? *Where* does it go? Only an approximate answer can be given to this question, but sufficient to throw light on certain general relations and ties of modern imperialism.

APPROXIMATE DISTRIBUTION OF FOREIGN CAPITAL
(ABOUT 1910)

(In billions of marks)

CONTINENT	GT. BRITAIN	FRANCE	GERMANY	TOTAL
Europe	4	23	18	45
America	37	4	10	51
Asia, Africa and Australia	29	8	7	44
Total	70	35	35	140

The principal spheres of investment of British capital are the British colonies, which are very large also in America (for example, Canada) not to mention Asia, etc. In this case, enormous exports of capital are bound up with the possession of enormous colonies, of the importance of which for imperialism we shall speak later. In regard to France, the situation is quite different. French capital exports are invested mainly in Europe, particularly in Russia (at

wirtschaft (Problems of World Economy), Jena, 1912, p. 235 et seq.; Dr. Sigmund Schilder, Entwicklungstendenzen der Weltwirtschaft (Trends of Development of World Economy), Berlin, 1912, Vol. I, p. 150; George Paish, Great Britain's Capital Investments, etc., in Journal of the Royal Statistical Society, Vol. LXXIV, 1910-11, p. 167; Georges Diouritch, L'expansion des banques allemandes à l'étranger, ses rapports avec le développement économique de l'Allemagne (Expansion of German Banks Abroad, in Connection with the Economic Development of Germany), Paris, 1909, p. 84.

least ten billion francs). This is mainly *loan* capital, in the form of government loans and not investments in industrial undertakings. Unlike British colonial imperialism, French imperialism might be termed usury imperialism. In regard to Germany, we have a third type; the German colonies are inconsiderable, and German capital invested abroad is divided fairly evenly between Europe and America.

The export of capital greatly affects and accelerates the development of capitalism in those countries to which it is exported. While, therefore, the export of capital may tend to a certain extent to arrest development in the countries exporting capital, it can only do so by expanding and deepening the further development of capitalism throughout the world.

The countries which export capital are nearly always able to obtain "advantages," the character of which throws light on the peculiarities of the epoch of finance capital and monopoly. The following passage, for instance, occurred in the Berlin review, *Die Bank,* for October 1913:

"A comedy worthy of the pen of Aristophanes is being played just now on the international capital market. Numerous foreign countries, from Spain to the Balkan states, from Russia to the Argentine, Brazil and China, are openly or secretly approaching the big money markets demanding loans, some of which are very urgent. The money market is not at the moment very bright and the political outlook is not yet promising. But not a single money market dares to refuse a foreign loan for fear that its neighbour might first anticipate it and so secure some small reciprocal service. In these international transactions the creditor nearly always manages to get some special advantages: an advantage of a commercial-political nature, a coaling station, a contract to construct a harbour, a fat concession, or an order for guns." [2]

Finance capital has created the epoch of monopolies, and monopolies introduce everywhere monopolist methods: the utilisation of "connections" for profitable transactions takes the place of competition on the open market. The most usual thing is to stipulate that part of the loan that is granted shall be spent on purchases in the country of issue, particularly on orders for war materials,

[2] *Die Bank,* 1913, pp. 1024-25.

or for ships, etc. In the course of the last two decades (1890-1910), France often resorted to this method. The export of capital abroad thus becomes a means for encouraging the export of commodities. In these circumstances transactions between particularly big firms assume a form "bordering on corruption," as Schilder [3] "delicately" puts it. Krupp in Germany, Schneider in France, Armstrong in England are instances of firms which have close connections with powerful banks and governments and cannot be "ignored" when arranging a loan.

France granted loans to Russia in 1905 and by the commercial treaty of September 16, 1905, she "squeezed" concessions out of her to run till 1917. She did the same thing when the Franco-Japanese commercial treaty was concluded on August 19, 1911. The tariff war between Austria and Serbia, which lasted with a seven months' interval, from 1906 to 1911, was partly caused by competition between Austria and France for supplying Serbia with war materials. In January 1912, Paul Deschanel stated in the Chamber of Deputies that from 1908 to 1911 French firms had supplied war materials to Serbia to the value of 45,000,000 francs.

A report from the Austro-Hungarian Consul at Sao-Paulo (Brazil) states:

"The construction of the Brazilian railways is being carried out chiefly by French, Belgian, British and German capital. In the financial operations connected with the construction of these railways the countries involved also stipulate for orders for the necessary railway materials."

Thus, finance capital, almost literally, one might say, spreads its net over all countries of the world. Banks founded in the colonies, or their branches, play an important part in these operations. German imperialists look with envy on the "old" colonising nations which are "well established" in this respect. In 1904, Great Britain had 50 colonial banks with 2,279 branches (in 1910 there were 72 banks with 5,449 branches); France had 20 with 136 branches; Holland 16 with 68 branches; and Germany had a "mere" 13 with

[3] Schilder, op. cit., Vol. I, pp. 346, 350 and 371.

70 branches.[4] The American capitalists, in their turn, are jealous of the English and German: "In South America," they complained in 1915, "five German banks have forty branches and five English banks have seventy branches.... England and Germany have invested in Argentina, Brazil, and Uruguay in the last twenty-five years approximately four thousand million dollars, and as a result enjoy together 46 per cent of the total trade of these three countries."[5]

The capital exporting countries have divided the world among themselves in the figurative sense of the term. But finance capital has also led to the *actual* division of the world.

[4] Riesser, *op. cit.*, fourth edition, pp. 374-75; Diouritch, p. 283.

[5] *The Annals of the American Academy of Political and Social Science,* Vol. LIX, May 1915, p. 301. In the same volume on p. 331, we read that the well-known statistician Paish, in the last annual issue of the financial magazine *Statist,* estimated the amount of capital exported by England, Germany, France, Belgium and Holland at 40,000,000,000 dollars, *i.e.,* 200,000,000,000 francs.

CHAPTER V

The Division of the World Among
Capitalist Combines

MONOPOLIST capitalist combines—cartels, syndicates, trusts—divide among themselves, first of all, the whole internal market of a country, and impose their control, more or less completely, upon the industry of that country. But under capitalism the home market is inevitably bound up with the foreign market. Capitalism long ago created a world market. As the export of capital increased, and as the foreign and colonial relations and the "spheres of influence" of the big monopolist combines expanded, things "naturally" gravitated towards an international agreement among these combines, and towards the formation of international cartels.

This is a new stage of world concentration of capital and production, incomparably higher than the preceding stages. Let us see how this super-monopoly develops.

The electrical industry is the most typical of the modern technical achievements of capitalism of the *end* of the nineteenth and beginning of the twentieth centuries. This industry has developed most in the two most advanced of the new capitalist countries, the United States and Germany. In Germany, the crisis of 1900 gave a particularly strong impetus to its concentration. During the crisis, the banks, which by this time had become fairly well merged with industry, greatly accelerated and deepened the collapse of relatively small firms and their absorption by the large ones.

"The banks," writes Jeidels, "in refusing a helping hand to the very companies which are in greatest need of capital bring on first a frenzied boom and then the hopeless failure of the companies which have not been attached to them closely long enough." [1]

As a result, after 1900, concentration in Germany proceeded by leaps and bounds. Up to 1900 there had been seven or eight

[1] Jeidels, *op. cit.*, p. 232.

"groups" in the electrical industry. Each was formed of several companies (altogether there were twenty-eight) and each was supported by from two to eleven banks. Between 1908 and 1912 all the groups were merged into two, or possibly one. The diagram below shows the process:

GROUPS IN THE GERMAN ELECTRICAL INDUSTRY

Prior to 1900:	FELTEN & GUILLAUME	LAH-MEYER	UNION A.E.G.	SIEMENS SCHUCKERT & HALSKE & CO.	BERG-MANN	KUM-MER
	FELTEN & LAHMEYER		A.E.G.	SIEMENS & HALSKE-SCHUCKERT	BERG-MANN	Failed in 1900
By 1912:	A.E.G. (GENERAL ELECTRIC CO.)			SIEMENS & HALSKE-SCHUCKERT		

(In close "co-operation" since 1908)

The famous A.E.G. (General Electric Company), which grew up in this way, controls 175 to 200 companies (through shareholdings), and a total capital of approximately 1,500,000,000 marks. Abroad, it has thirty-four direct agencies, of which twelve are joint stock companies, in more than ten countries. As early as 1904 the amount of capital invested abroad by the German electrical industry was estimated at 233,000,000 marks. Of this sum, 62,000,000 were invested in Russia. Needless to say, the A.E.G. is a huge combine. Its manufacturing companies alone number no less than sixteen, and their factories make the most varied articles, from cables and insulators to motor cars and aeroplanes.

But concentration in Europe was a part of the process of concentration in America, which developed in the following way:

GENERAL ELECTRIC COMPANY

United States:	Thomson-Houston Co. establishes a firm in Europe	Edison Co. establishes in Europe the French Edison Co. which transfers its patents to the German firm
Germany:		Gen'l Electric Co.
	Union Electric Co.	(A.E.G.)

GENERAL ELECTRIC CO. (A.E.G.)

Thus, *two* "Great Powers" in the electrical industry were formed. "There are no other electric companies in the world *completely* independent of them," wrote Heinig in his article "The Path of the Electric Trust." An idea, although far from complete, of the turnover and the size of the enterprises of the two "trusts" can be obtained from the following figures:

		TURNOVER (*mill. marks*)	NO. OF EMPLOYEES	NET PROFITS (*mill. marks*)
AMERICA:				
General Electric Co.	1907	252	28,000	35.4
	1910	298	32,000	45.6
GERMANY: A.E.G.	1907	216	30,700	14.5
	1911	362	60,800	21.7

In 1907, the German and American trusts concluded an agreement by which they divided the world between themselves. Competition between them ceased. The American General Electric Company "got" the United States and Canada. The A.E.G. "got" Germany, Austria, Russia, Holland, Denmark, Switzerland, Turkey and the Balkans. Special agreements, naturally secret, were concluded regarding the penetration of "subsidiary" companies into new branches of industry, into "new" countries formally not yet allotted. The two trusts were to exchange inventions and experiments.[2]

It is easy to understand how difficult competition has become against this trust, which is practically world-wide, which controls a capital of several billion, and has its "branches," agencies, representatives, connections, etc., in every corner of the world. But the division of the world between two powerful trusts does not remove the possibility of *redivision,* if the relation of forces changes as a result of uneven development, war, bankruptcy, etc.

The oil industry provides an instructive example of attempts at such a redivision, or rather of a struggle for redivision.

"The world oil market," wrote Jeidels in 1905, "is even today divided in the main between two great financial groups—Rockefeller's American Standard Oil Co., and the controlling interests of the Russian oil-fields in Baku, Rothschild and Nobel. The two groups are in close alliance. But for several years, five enemies have been threatening their monopoly:"[3]

[2] Riesser, *op. cit.;* Diouritch, *op. cit.,* p. 239; Kurt Heinig, *op. cit,*

[3] Jeidels, *op. cit.,* pp. 192-93.

1) The exhaustion of the American oil wells; [4] 2) the competition of the firm of Mantashev of Baku; 3) the Austrian wells; 4) the Rumanian wells; 5) the overseas oilfields, particularly in the Dutch colonies (the extremely rich firms, Samuel and Shell, also connected with British capital). The three last groups are connected with the great German banks, principally, the Deutsche Bank. These banks independently and systematically developed the oil industry in Rumania, in order to have a foothold of their "own." In 1907, 185,000,000 francs of foreign capital were invested in the Rumanian oil industry, of which 74,000,000 came from Germany.[5]

A struggle began, which in economic literature is fittingly called "the struggle for the division of the world." On one side, the Rockefeller trust, wishing to conquer *everything,* formed a subsidiary company *right in* Holland, and bought up oil wells in the Dutch Indies, in order to strike at its principal enemy, the Anglo-Dutch Shell trust. On the other side, the Deutsche Bank and the other German banks aimed at "retaining" Rumania "for themselves" and at uniting it with Russia against Rockefeller. The latter controlled far more capital and an excellent system of oil transport and distribution. The struggle had to end, and did end in 1907, with the utter defeat of the Deutsche Bank, which was confronted with the alternative: either to liquidate its oil business and lose millions, or to submit. It chose to submit, and concluded a very disadvantageous agreement with the American trust. The Deutsche Bank agreed "not to attempt anything which might injure American interests." Provision was made, however, for the annulment of the agreement in the event of Germany establishing a state oil monopoly.

Then the "comedy of oil" began. One of the German finance kings, von Gwinner, a director of the Deutsche Bank, began through his private secretary, Strauss, a campaign *for* a state oil monopoly. The gigantic machine of the big German bank and all its wide "connections" were set in motion. The press bubbled over with "patriotic" indignation against the "yoke" of the American trust, and, on March 15, 1911, the Reichstag by an almost unanimous vote, adopted a motion asking the government to intro-

[4] In Pennsylvania, chief oil region in U. S. at time of Jeidel's study.—*Ed.*
[5] Diouritch, *op. cit.,* p. 245.

duce a bill for the establishment of an oil monopoly. The government seized upon this "popular" idea, and the game of the Deutsche Bank, which hoped to cheat its American partner and improve its business by a state monopoly, appeared to have been won. The German oil magnates saw visions of wonderful profits, which would not be less than those of the Russian sugar refiners. ... But, firstly, the big German banks quarrelled among themselves over the division of the spoils. The Disconto-Gesellschaft exposed the covetous aims of the Deutsche Bank; secondly, the government took fright at the prospect of a struggle with Rockefeller; it was doubtful whether Germany could be sure of obtaining oil from other sources. (The Rumanian output was small.) Thirdly, just at that time the 1913 credits of a billion marks were voted for Germany's war preparations. The project of the oil monopoly was postponed. The Rockefeller trust came out of the struggle, for the time being, victorious.

The Berlin review, *Die Bank*, said in this connection that Germany could only fight the oil trust by establishing an electricity monopoly and by converting water power into cheap electricity.

"But," the author added, "the electricity monopoly will come when the producers need it, that is to say, on the eve of the next great crash in the electrical industry, and when the powerful, expensive electric stations which are now being put up at great cost everywhere by private electrical concerns, which obtain partial monopolies from the state, from towns, etc., can no longer work at a profit. Water power will then have to be used. But it will be impossible to convert it into cheap electricity at state expense; it will have to be handed over to a 'private monopoly controlled by the state,' because of the immense compensation and damages that would have to be paid to private industry.... So it was with the nitrate monopoly, so it is with the oil monopoly; so it will be with the electric power monopoly. It is time for our state socialists, who allow themselves to be blinded by beautiful principles, to understand once and for all that in Germany monopolies have never pursued the aim, nor have they had the result, of benefiting the consumer, or of handing over to the state part of the *entrepreneurs'* profits; they have served only to facilitate, at the expense of the state, the recovery of private industries which were on the verge of bankruptcy." [6]

[6] *Die Bank*, 1912, p. 1036; *cf.* also *ibid.*, p. 629 *et seq.;* 1913, I, p. 388.

Such are the valuable admissions which the German bourgeois economists are forced to make. We see plainly here how private monopolies and state monopolies are bound up together in the age of finance capital; how both are but separate links in the imperialist struggle between the big monopolists for the division of the world.

In mercantile shipping, the tremendous development of concentration has ended also in the division of the world. In Germany two powerful companies have raised themselves to first rank, the Hamburg-Amerika and the Norddeutscher Lloyd, each having a capital of 200,000,000 marks (in stocks and bonds) and possessing 185 to 189 million marks worth of shipping tonnage. On the other side, in America, on January 1, 1903, the Morgan trust, the International Mercantile Marine Co., was formed which united nine British and American steamship companies, and which controlled a capital of 120,000,000 dollars (480,000,000 marks). As early as 1903, the German giants and the Anglo-American trust concluded an agreement and divided the world in accordance with the division of profits. The German companies undertook not to compete in the Anglo-American traffic. The ports were carefully "allotted" to each; a joint committee of control was set up, etc. This contract was concluded for twenty years, with the prudent provision for its annulment in the event of war.[7]

Extremely instructive also is the story of the creation of the International Rail Cartel. The first attempt of the British, Belgian and German rail manufacturers to create such a cartel was made as early as 1884, at the time of a severe industrial depression. The manufacturers agreed not to compete with one another for the home markets of the countries involved, and they divided the foreign markets in the following quotas: Great Britain 66 per cent; Germany 27 per cent; Belgium 7 per cent. India was reserved entirely for Great Britain. Joint war was declared against a British firm which remained outside the cartel. The cost of this economic war was met by a percentage levy on all sales. But in 1886 the cartel collapsed when two British firms retired from it. It is characteristic that agreement could not be achieved in the period of industrial prosperity which followed.

[7] Riesser, *op. cit.*, p. 125.

At the beginning of 1904, the German steel syndicate was formed. In November 1904, the International Rail Cartel was revived, with the following quotas for foreign trade: England 53.5 per cent; Germany 28.83 per cent; Belgium 17.67 per cent. France came in later with 4.8 per cent, 5.8 per cent and 6.4 per cent in the first, second and third years respectively, in excess of the 100 per cent limit, *i.e.*, when the total was 104.8 per cent, etc. In 1905, the United States Steel Corporation entered the cartel; then Austria; then Spain.

"At the present time," wrote Vogelstein in 1910, "the division of the world is completed, and the big consumers, primarily the state railways—since the world has been parcelled out without consideration for their interests—can now dwell like the poet in the heaven of Jupiter." [8]

We will mention also the International Zinc Syndicate, established in 1909, which carefully apportioned output among three groups of factories: German, Belgian, French, Spanish and British. Then there is the International Dynamite Trust, of which Liefmann says that it is

"quite a modern, close alliance of all the manufacturers of explosives who, with the French and American dynamite manufacturers who have organised in a similar manner, have divided the whole world among themselves, so to speak." [9]

Liefmann calculated that in 1897 there were altogether about forty international cartels in which Germany had a share, while in 1910 there were about a hundred.

Certain bourgeois writers (with whom K. Kautsky, who has completely abandoned the Marxist position he held, for example, in 1909, has now associated himself) express the opinion that international cartels are the most striking expressions of the internationalisation of capital, and, therefore, give the hope of peace among nations under capitalism. Theoretically, this opinion is absurd, while in practice it is sophistry and a dishonest defence of the worst opportunism. International cartels show to what point

[8] Th. Vogelstein, *Organisationsformen (Forms of Organisation)*, p. 100.
[9] R. Liefmann, *Kartelle und Trusts*, second ed., p. 161.

capitalist monopolies have developed, and they *reveal the object* of the struggle between the various capitalist groups. This last circumstance is the most important; it alone shows us the historico-economic significance of events; for the *forms* of the struggle may and do constantly change in accordance with varying, relatively particular, and temporary causes, but the *essence* of the struggle, its class *content, cannot* change while classes exist. It is easy to understand, for example, that it is in the interests of the German bourgeoisie, whose theoretical arguments have now been adopted by Kautsky (we will deal with this later), to obscure the *content* of the present economic struggle (the division of the world) and to emphasise this or that *form* of the struggle. Kautsky makes the same mistake. Of course, we have in mind not only the German bourgeoisie, but the bourgeoisie all over the world. The capitalists divide the world, not out of any particular malice, but because the degree of concentration which has been reached forces them to adopt this method in order to get profits. And they divide it in proportion to "capital," in proportion to "strength," because there cannot be any other system of division under commodity production and capitalism. But strength varies with the degree of economic and political development. In order to understand what takes place, it is necessary to know what questions are settled by this change of forces. The question as to whether these changes are "purely" economic or *non*-economic (*e.g.,* military) is a secondary one, which does not in the least affect the fundamental view on the latest epoch of capitalism. To substitute for the question of the *content* of the struggle and agreements between capitalist combines the question of the *form* of these struggles and agreements (today peaceful, tomorrow war-like, the next day war-like again) is to sink to the role of a sophist.

The epoch of modern capitalism shows us that certain relations are established between capitalist alliances, *based* on the economic division of the world; while parallel with this fact and in connection with it, certain relations are established between political alliances, between states, on the basis of the territorial division of the world, of the struggle for colonies, of the "struggle for economic territory."

CHAPTER VI

The Division of the World Among
the Great Powers

In his book, *The Territorial Development of the European Colonies*, A. Supan,[1] the geographer, gives the following brief summary of this development at the end of the nineteenth century:

PERCENTAGE OF TERRITORIES BELONGING TO THE EUROPEAN COLONIAL POWERS (*Including United States*)

	1876	1900	INCREASE OR DECREASE
Africa	10.8	90.4	+ 79.6
Polynesia	56.8	98.9	+ 42.1
Asia	51.5	56.6	+ 5.1
Australia	100.0	100.0	—
America	27.5	27.2	— 0.3

"The characteristic feature of this period," he concludes, "is therefore, the division of Africa and Polynesia."

As there are no unoccupied territories—that is, territories that do not belong to any state—in Asia and America, Mr. Supan's conclusion must be carried further, and we must say that the characteristic feature of this period is the final partition of the globe—not in the sense that a *new* partition is impossible—on the contrary, new partitions are possible and inevitable—but in the sense that the colonial policy of the capitalist countries has *completed* the seizure of the unoccupied territories on our planet. For the first time the world is completely divided up, so that in the future *only* redivision is possible; territories can only pass from one "owner" to another, instead of passing as unowned territory to an "owner."

Hence, we are passing through a peculiar period of world colonial

[1] A. Supan, *Die territoriale Entwicklung der europäischen Kolonien,* Gotha, 1906, p. 254.

policy, which is closely associated with the "latest stage in the development of capitalism," with finance capital. For this reason, it is essential first of all to deal in detail with the facts, in order to ascertain exactly what distinguishes this period from those preceding it, and what the present situation is. In the first place, two questions of fact arise here. Is an intensification of colonial policy, an intensification of the struggle for colonies, observed precisely in this period of finance capital? And how, in this respect, is the world divided at the present time?

The American writer, Morris, in his book on the history of colonisation,[2] has made an attempt to compile data on the colonial possessions of Great Britain, France and Germany during different periods of the nineteenth century. The following is a brief summary of the results he has obtained:

COLONIAL POSSESSIONS

(Million square miles and million inhabitants)

	GREAT BRITAIN		FRANCE		GERMANY	
	AREA	POP.	AREA	POP.	AREA	POP.
1815-30	?	126.4	0.02	0.5	—	—
1860	2.5	145.1	0.2	3.4	—	—
1880	7.7	267.9	0.7	7.5	—	—
1899	9.3	309.0	3.7	56.4	1.0	14.7

For Great Britain, the period of the enormous expansion of colonial conquests is that between 1860 and 1880, and it was also very considerable in the last twenty years of the nineteenth century. For France and Germany this period falls precisely in these last twenty years. We saw above that the apex of pre-monopoly capitalist development, of capitalism in which free competition was predominant, was reached in the 'sixties and 'seventies of the last century. We now see that it is *precisely after that period* that the "boom" in colonial annexations begins, and that the struggle for the territorial division of the world becomes extraordinarily keen. It is beyond doubt, therefore, that capitalism's transition to the

[2] Henry C. Morris, *The History of Colonisation*, New York, 1900, II, p. 88; I, pp. 304, 419.

stage of monopoly capitalism, to finance capital, is *bound up* with the intensification of the struggle for the partition of the world.

Hobson, in his work on imperialism, marks the years 1884-1900 as the period of the intensification of the colonial "expansion" of the chief European states. According to his estimate, Great Britain during these years acquired 3,700,000 square miles of territory with a population of 57,000,000; France acquired 3,600,000 square miles with a population of 36,500,000; Germany 1,000,000 square miles with a population of 16,700,000; Belgium 900,000 square miles with 30,000,000 inhabitants; Portugal 800,000 square miles with 9,000,000 inhabitants. The quest for colonies by all the capitalist states at the end of the nineteenth century and particularly since the 1880's is a commonly known fact in the history of diplomacy and of foreign affairs.

When free competition in Great Britain was at its zenith, *i.e.,* between 1840 and 1860, the leading British bourgeois politicians were opposed to colonial policy and were of the opinion that the liberation of the colonies and their complete separation from Britain was inevitable and desirable. M. Beer, in an article, "Modern British Imperialism," [3] published in 1898, shows that in 1852, Disraeli, a statesman generally inclined towards imperialism, declared: "The colonies are millstones round our necks." But at the end of the nineteenth century the heroes of the hour in England were Cecil Rhodes and Joseph Chamberlain, open advocates of imperialism, who applied the imperialist policy in the most cynical manner.

It is not without interest to observe that even at that time these leading British bourgeois politicians fully appreciated the connection between what might be called the purely economic and the politico-social roots of modern imperialism. Chamberlain advocated imperialism by calling it a "true, wise and economical policy," and he pointed particularly to the German, American and Belgian competition which Great Britain was encountering in the world market. Salvation lies in monopolies, said the capitalists as they formed cartels, syndicates and trusts. Salvation lies in monopolies, echoed the political leaders of the bourgeoisie, hastening to appro-

[3] *Die Neue Zeit,* XVI, I, 1898, p. 302.

priate the parts of the world not yet shared out. The journalist, Stead, relates the following remarks uttered by his close friend Cecil Rhodes, in 1895, regarding his imperialist ideas:

"I was in the East End of London yesterday and attended a meeting of the unemployed. I listened to the wild speeches, which were just a cry for 'bread,' 'bread,' 'bread,' and on my way home I pondered over the scene and I became more than ever convinced of the importance of imperialism.... My cherished idea is a solution for the social problem, *i.e.*, in order to save the 40,000,000 inhabitants of the United Kingdom from a bloody civil war, we colonial statesmen must acquire new lands to settle the surplus population, to provide new markets for the goods produced by them in the factories and mines. The Empire, as I have always said, is a bread and butter question. If you want to avoid civil war, you must become imperialists." [4]

This is what Cecil Rhodes, millionaire, king of finance, the man who was mainly responsible for the Boer War, said in 1895. His defence of imperialism is just crude and cynical, but in substance it does not differ from the "theory" advocated by Messrs. Maslov, Südekum, Potresov, David, and the founder of Russian Marxism and others. Cecil Rhodes was a somewhat more honest social-chauvinist.

To tabulate as exactly as possible the territorial division of the world, and the changes which have occurred during the last decades, we will take the data furnished by Supan in the work already quoted on the colonial possessions of all the powers of the world. Supan examines the years 1876 and 1900; we will take the year 1876—a year aptly selected, for it is precisely at that time that the pre-monopolist stage of development of West European capitalism can be said to have been completed, in the main, and we will take the year 1914, and in place of Supan's figures we will quote the more recent statistics of Hübner's *Geographical and Statistical Tables*. Supan gives figures only for colonies: we think it useful in order to present a complete picture of the division of the world to add brief figures on non-colonial and semi-colonial countries like Persia, China and Turkey. Persia is already almost

[4] *Ibid.*, p. 304.

completely a colony; China and Turkey are on the way to becoming colonies. We thus get the following summary:

COLONIAL POSSESSIONS OF THE GREAT POWERS

(Million square kilometres and million inhabitants)

| | COLONIES | | | | HOME COUNTRIES | | TOTAL | |
| | 1876 | | 1914 | | 1914 | | 1914 | |
	AREA	POP.	AREA	POP.	AREA	POP.	AREA	POP.
Great Britain	22.5	251.9	33.5	393.5	0.3	46.5	33.8	440.0
Russia	17.0	15.9	17.4	33.2	5.4	136.2	22.8	169.4
France	0.9	6.0	10.6	55.5	0.5	39.6	11.1	95.1
Germany	—	—	2.9	12.3	0.5	64.9	3.4	77.2
U.S.A.	—	—	0.3	9.7	9.4	97.0	9.7	106.7
Japan	—	—	0.3	19.2	0.4	53.0	0.7	72.2
Total	40.4	273.8	65.0	523.4	16.5	437.2	81.5	960.6
Colonies of other powers (Belgium, Holland, etc.)							9.9	45.3
Semi-colonial countries (Persia, China, Turkey)							14.5	361.2
Other countries							28.0	289.9
Total area and population of the world							133.9	1,657.0

We see from these figures how "complete" was the partition of the world at the end of the nineteenth and beginning of the twentieth centuries. After 1876 colonial possessions increased to an enormous degree, more than one and a half times, from 40,000,000 to 65,000,000 square kilometres in area for the six biggest powers, an increase of 25,000,000 square kilometres, that is, one and a half times greater than the area of the "home" countries, which have a total of 16,500,000 square kilometres. In 1876 three powers had no colonies, and a fourth, France, had scarcely any. In 1914 these four powers had 14,100,000 square kilometres of colonies, or an area one and a half times greater than that of Europe, with a population of nearly 100,000,000. The unevenness in the rate of expansion of colonial possessions is very marked. If, for instance, we compare France, Germany and Japan, which do not differ very much in area and population, we will see that the first has annexed almost three times as much colonial territory as the other two combined. In regard to finance capital, also, France, at the beginning of the period we are considering, was perhaps several times richer than Germany and Japan put together. In addition to, and on the basis of, purely economic causes, geographical conditions and other factors also affect the dimensions of colonial possessions. However strong the process of levelling the world, of levelling the economic and living conditions in different countries, may have been in the past decades as a result of the pressure of large-scale industry, exchange and finance capital, great differences still remain; and among the six powers, we see, firstly, young capitalist powers (America, Germany, Japan) which progressed very rapidly; secondly, countries with an old capitalist development (France and Great Britain), which, of late, have made much slower progress than the previously mentioned countries, and, thirdly, a country (Russia) which is economically most backward, in which modern capitalist imperialism is enmeshed, so to speak, in a particularly close network of pre-capitalist relations.

Alongside the colonial possessions of these great powers, we have placed the small colonies of the small states, which are, so to speak, the next possible and probable objects of a new colonial "share-out." Most of these little states are able to retain their colonies only because of the conflicting interests, frictions, etc., among the big powers, which prevent them from coming to an agreement in regard to the division of the spoils. The "semi-colonial states" provide an example of the transitional forms which are to be found in all spheres of nature and society. Finance capital is such a great, it may be said, such a decisive force in all economic and international relations, that it is capable of subordinating to itself, and actually does subordinate to itself, even states enjoying complete political independence. We shall shortly see examples of this. Naturally, however, finance capital finds it most "convenient," and is able to extract the greatest profit from a subordination which involves the loss of the political independence of the subjected countries and peoples. In this connection, the semi-colonial countries provide a typical example of the "middle stage." It is natural that the struggle for these semi-dependent countries should have become particularly bitter during the period of finance capital, when the rest of the world had already been divided up.

Colonial policy and imperialism existed before this latest stage of capitalism, and even before capitalism. Rome, founded on slavery, pursued a colonial policy and achieved imperialism. But "general" arguments about imperialism, which ignore, or put into the background the fundamental difference of social-economic systems, inevitably degenerate into absolutely empty banalities, or into grandiloquent comparisons like "Greater Rome and Greater Britain." [5] Even the colonial policy of capitalism in its *previous* stages is essentially different from the colonial policy of finance capital.

The principal feature of modern capitalism is the domination of monopolist combines of the big capitalists. These monopolies are most firmly established when *all* the sources of raw materials are controlled by the one group. And we have seen with what zeal the international capitalist combines exert every effort to make it impossible for their rivals to compete with them; for example, by buying up mineral lands, oil fields, etc. Colonial possession alone gives complete guarantee of success to the monopolies against all the risks of the struggle with competitors, including the risk that the latter will defend themselves by means of a law establishing a state monopoly. The more capitalism is developed, the more the need for raw materials is felt, the more bitter competition becomes, and the more feverishly the hunt for raw materials proceeds throughout the whole world, the more desperate becomes the struggle for the acquisition of colonies

Schilder writes:

"It may even be asserted, although it may sound paradoxical to some, that in the more or less discernible future the growth of the urban industrial population is more likely to be hindered by a shortage of raw materials for industry than by a shortage of food."

For example, there is a growing shortage of timber—the price of which is steadily rising—of leather, and raw materials for the textile industry.

[5] A reference to the book by C. P. Lucas, *Greater Rome and Greater Britain,* Oxford 1912, or the Earl of Cromer's *Ancient and Modern Imperialism,* London, 1910.

"As instances of the efforts of associations of manufacturers to create an equilibrium between industry and agriculture in world economy as a whole, we might mention the International Federation of Cotton Spinners' Associations in the most important industrial countries, founded in 1904, and the European Federation of Flax Spinners' Associations, founded on the same model in 1910."[6]

The bourgeois reformists, and among them particularly the present-day adherents of Kautsky, of course, try to belittle the importance of facts of this kind by arguing that it "would be possible" to obtain raw materials in the open market without a "costly and dangerous" colonial policy; and that it would be "possible" to increase the supply of raw materials to an enormous extent "simply" by improving agriculture. But these arguments are merely an apology for imperialism, an attempt to embellish it, because they ignore the principal feature of modern capitalism: monopoly. Free markets are becoming more and more a thing of the past; monopolist syndicates and trusts are restricting them more and more every day, and "simply" improving agriculture reduces itself to improving the conditions of the masses, to raising wages and reducing profits. Where, except in the imagination of the sentimental reformists, are there any trusts capable of interesting themselves in the condition of the masses instead of the conquest of colonies?

Finance capital is not only interested in the already known sources of raw materials; it is also interested in potential sources of raw materials, because present-day technical development is extremely rapid, and because land which is useless today may be made fertile tomorrow if new methods are applied (to devise these new methods a big bank can equip a whole expedition of engineers, agricultural experts, etc.), and large amounts of capital are invested. This also applies to prospecting for minerals, to new methods of working up and utilising raw materials, etc., etc. Hence, the inevitable striving of finance capital to extend its economic territory and even its territory in general. In the same way that the trusts capitalise their property by estimating it at two or three times its value, taking into account its "potential" (and

[6] Schilder, *op. cit.*, pp. 38 and 42.

not present) returns, and the further results of monopoly, so finance capital strives to seize the largest possible amount of land of all kinds and in any place it can, and by any means, counting on the possibilities of finding raw materials there, and fearing to be left behind in the insensate struggle for the last available scraps of undivided territory, or for the repartition of that which has been already divided.

The British capitalists are exerting every effort to develop cotton growing in *their* colony, Egypt (in 1904, out of 2,300,000 hectares of land under cultivation, 600,000, or more than one-fourth, were devoted to cotton growing); the Russians are doing the same in *their* colony, Turkestan; and they are doing so because in this way they will be in a better position to defeat their foreign competitors, to monopolise the sources of raw materials and form a more economical and profitable textile trust in which *all* the processes of cotton production and manufacturing will be "combined" and concentrated in the hands of a single owner.

The necessity of exporting capital also gives an impetus to the conquest of colonies, for in the colonial market it is easier to eliminate competition, to make sure of orders, to strengthen the necessary "connections," etc., by monoplist methods (and sometimes it is the only possible way).

The non-economic superstructure which grows up on the basis of finance capital, its politics and its ideology, stimulates the striving for colonial conquest. "Finance capital does not want liberty, it wants domination," as Hilferding very truly says. And a French bourgeois writer, developing and supplementing, as it were, the ideas of Cecil Rhodes, which we quoted above, writes that social causes should be added to the economic causes of modern colonial policy.

"Owing to the growing difficulties of life which weigh not only on the masses of the workers, but also on the middle classes, impatience, irritation and hatred are accumulating in all the countries of the old civilisation and are becoming a menace to public order; employment must be found for the energy which is being hurled out of the definite class channel; it must be given an outlet abroad in order to avert an explosion at home."[7]

Since we are speaking of colonial policy in the period of capitalist imperialism, it must be observed that finance capital and its corresponding foreign policy, which reduces itself to the struggle of the Great Powers for the economic and political division of the world, give rise to a number of *transitional* forms of national dependence. The division of the world into two main groups—of colony-owning countries on the one hand and colonies on the other—is not the only typical feature of this period; there is also a variety of forms of dependent countries; countries which, officially, are politically independent, but which are, in fact, enmeshed in the net of financial and diplomatic dependence. We have already referred to one form of dependence—the semi-colony. Another example is provided by Argentina.

"South America, and especially Argentina," writes Schulze-Gaevernitz in his work on British imperialism, "is so dependent financially on London that it ought to be described as almost a British commercial colony."[8]

Basing himself on the report of the Austro-Hungarian consul at Buenos Aires for 1909, Schilder estimates the amount of British capital invested in Argentina at 8,750,000,000 francs. It is not difficult to imagine the solid bonds that are thus created between British finance capital (and its faithful "friend," diplomacy) and the Argentine bourgeoisie, with the leading businessmen and politicians of that country.

A somewhat different form of financial and diplomatic dependence, accompanied by political independence, is presented by Portugal. Portugal is an independent sovereign state. In actual fact, however, for more than two hundred years, since the war of the

---

[7] Wahl, *La France aux colonies* (*France in the Colonies*), quoted by Henri Bussier, *Le partage de l'Océanie* (*The Partition of Oceania*), Paris, 1905, pp. 165-66.

[8] Schulze-Gaevernitz, *Britischer Imperialismus und englischer Freihandel zu Beginn des 20. Jahrhunderts* (*British Imperialism and English Free Trade at the Beginning of the Twentieth Century*), Leipzig, 1906, p. 318. Sartorius von Waltershausen says the same in *Das volkswirtschaftliche System der Kapitalanlage im Auslande* (*The National Economic System of Capital Investments Abroad*), Berlin, 1907, p. 46.

Spanish Succession (1700-14), it has been a British protectorate. Great Britain has protected Portugal and her colonies in order to fortify her own positions in the fight against her rivals, Spain and France. In return she has received commercial advantages, preferential import of goods, and, above all, of capital into Portugal and the Portuguese colonies, the right to use the ports and islands of Portugal, her telegraph cables, etc.[9] Relations of this kind have always existed between big and little states. But during the period of capitalist imperialism they become a general system, they form part of the process of "dividing the world"; they become a link in the chain of operations of world finance capital.

In order to complete our examination of the question of the division of the world, we must make the following observation. This question was raised quite openly and definitely not only in American literature after the Spanish-American War, and in English literature after the Boer War, at the very end of the nineteenth century and the beginning of the twentieth; not only has German literature, which always "jealously" watches "British imperialism," systematically given its appraisal of this fact, but it has also been raised in French bourgeois literature in terms as wide and clear as they can be made from the bourgeois point of view. We will quote Driault, the historian, who, in his book, *Political and Social Problems at the End of the Nineteenth Century,* in the chapter "The Great Powers and the Division of the World," wrote the following:

"During recent years, all the free territory of the globe, with the exception of China, has been occupied by the powers of Europe and North America. Several conflicts and displacements of influence have already occurred over this matter, which foreshadow more terrible outbreaks in the near future. For it is necessary to make haste. The nations which have not yet made provisions for themselves run the risk of never receiving their share and never participating in the tremendous exploitation of the globe which will be one of the essential features of the next century" (*i.e.,* the twentieth). "That is why all Europe and America has lately been afflicted with the fever of colonial

[9] Schilder, *op. cit.,* Vol. I, pp. 159-61.

expansion, of 'imperialism,' that most characteristic feature of the end of the nineteenth century."

And the author added:

"In this partition of the world, in this furious pursuit of the treasures and of the big markets of the globe, the relative power of the empires founded in this nineteenth century is totally out of proportion to the place occupied in Europe by the nations which founded them. The dominant powers in Europe, those which decide the destinies of the Continent, are *not* equally preponderant in the whole world. And, as colonial power, the hope of controlling hitherto unknown wealth, will obviously react to influence the relative strength of the European powers, the colonial question—'imperialism,' if you will—which has already modified the political conditions of Europe, will modify them more and more." [10]

[10] Ed. Driault, *Problèmes politiques et sociaux*, Paris, 1907, p. 289.

CHAPTER VII

Imperialism as a Special Stage
of Capitalism

WE must now try to sum up and put together what has been said above on the subject of imperialism. Imperialism emerged as the development and direct continuation of the fundamental attributes of capitalism in general. But capitalism only became capitalist imperialism at a definite and very high stage of its development, when certain of its fundamental attributes began to be transformed into their opposites, when the features of a period of transition from capitalism to a higher social and economic system began to take shape and reveal themselves all along the line. Economically, the main thing in this process is the substitution of capitalist monopolies for capitalist free competition. Free competition is the fundamental attribute of capitalism, and of commodity production generally. Monopoly is exactly the opposite of free competition; but we have seen the latter being transformed into monopoly before our very eyes, creating large-scale industry and eliminating small industry, replacing large-scale industry by still larger-scale industry, finally leading to such a concentration of production and capital that monopoly has been and is the result: cartels, syndicates and trusts, and merging with them, the capital of a dozen or so banks manipulating thousands of millions. At the same time monopoly, which has grown out of free competition, does not abolish the latter, but exists over it and alongside of it, and thereby gives rise to a number of very acute, intense antagonisms, friction and conflicts. Monopoly is the transition from capitalism to a higher system.

If it were necessary to give the briefest possible definition of imperialism we should have to say that imperialism is the monopoly stage of capitalism. Such a definition would include what is most important, for, on the one hand, finance capital is the bank capital of a few big monopolist banks, merged with the capital of the monopolist combines of manufacturers; and, on the other hand, the division of the world is the transition from a colonial policy which has extended without hindrance to territories unoccupied by any capitalist power, to a colonial policy of monopolistic possession of the territory of the world which has been completely divided up.

But very brief definitions, although convenient, for they sum up the main points, are nevertheless inadequate, because very important features of the phenomenon that has to be defined have to be especially deduced. And so, without forgetting the conditional and relative value of all definitions, which can never include all the concatenations of a phenomenon in its complete development, we must give a definition of imperialism that will embrace the following five essential features:

1) The concentration of production and capital developed to such a high stage that it created monopolies which play a decisive role in economic life.

2) The merging of bank capital with industrial capital, and the creation, on the basis of this "finance capital," of a "financial oligarchy.

3) The export of capital, which has become extremely important, as distinguished from the export of commodities.

4) The formation of international capitalist monopolies which share the world among themselves.

5) The territorial division of the whole world among the greatest capitalist powers is completed.

Imperialism is capitalism in that stage of development in which the dominance of monopolies and finance capital has established itself; in which the export of capital has acquired pronounced importance; in which the division of the world among the international trusts has begun; in which the division of all territories of the globe among the great capitalist powers has been completed.

We shall see later that imperialism can and must be defined differently if consideration is to be given, not only to the basic, purely economic factors—to which the above definition is limited—

but also to the historical place of this stage of capitalism in relation
to capitalism in general, or to the relations between imperialism
and the two main trends in the working class movement. The
point to be noted just now is that imperialism, as interpreted above,
undoubtedly represents a special stage in the development of capitalism. In order to enable the reader to obtain as well grounded
an idea of imperialism as possible, we deliberately quoted largely
from *bourgeois* economists who are obliged to admit the particularly incontrovertible facts regarding modern capitalist economy.
With the same object in view, we have produced detailed statistics which reveal the extent to which bank capital, etc., has
developed, showing how the transformation of quantity into quality, of developed capitalism into imperialism, has expressed itself.
Needless to say, all boundaries in nature and in society are conditional and changeable, and, consequently, it would be absurd
to discuss the exact year or the decade in which imperialism
"definitely" became established.

In this matter of defining imperialism, however, we have to enter
into controversy, primarily, with K. Kautsky, the principal Marxian
theoretician of the epoch of the so-called Second International—
that is, of the twenty-five years between 1889 and 1914.

Kautsky, in 1915 and even in November 1914, very emphatically
attacked the fundamental ideas expressed in our definition of
imperialism. Kautsky said that imperialism must not be regarded
as a "phase" or stage of economy, but as a policy; a definite policy
"preferred" by finance capital; that imperialism cannot be "identi-
fied" with "contemporary capitalism"; that if imperialism is to be
understood to mean "all the phenomena of contemporary capitalism"—cartels, protection, the domination of the financiers and
colonial policy—then the question as to whether imperialism is
necessary to capitalism becomes reduced to the "flattest tautology";
because, in that case, "imperialism is naturally a vital necessity for
capitalism," and so on. The best way to present Kautsky's ideas
is to quote his own definition of imperialism, which is diametrically
opposed to the substance of the ideas which we have set forth (for
the objections coming from the camp of the German Marxists,
who have been advocating such ideas for many years already, have

been long known to Kautsky as the objections of a definite trend in Marxism).

Kautsky's definition is as follows:

"Imperialism is a product of highly developed industrial capitalism. It consists in the striving of every industrial capitalist nation to bring under its control and to annex increasingly big *agrarian*" (Kautsky's italics) "regions irrespective of what nations inhabit those regions."[1]

This definition is utterly worthless because it one-sidedly, *i.e.,* arbitrarily, brings out the national question alone (although this is extremely important in itself as well as in its relation to imperialism), it arbitrarily and *inaccurately* relates this question *only* to industrial capital in the countries which annex other nations, and in an equally arbitrary and inaccurate manner brings out the annexation of agrarian regions.

Imperialism is a striving for annexations—this is what the *political* part of Kautsky's definition amounts to. It is correct, but very incomplete, for politically, imperialism is, in general, a striving towards violence and reaction. For the moment, however, we are interested in the *economic* aspect of the question, which Kautsky *himself* introduced into *his* definition. The inaccuracy of Kautsky's definition is strikingly obvious. The characteristic feature of imperialism is *not* industrial capital, *but* finance capital. It is not an accident that in France it was precisely the extraordinarily rapid development of *finance* capital, and the weakening of industrial capital, that, from 1880 onwards, gave rise to the extreme extension of annexationist (colonial) policy. The characteristic feature of imperialism is precisely that it strives to annex *not only* agricultural regions, but even highly industrialised regions (German appetite for Belgium; French appetite for Lorraine), because 1) the fact that the world is already divided up obliges those contemplating a *new* division to reach out for *any kind* of territory, and 2) because an essential feature of imperialism is the rivalry between a number of great powers in the striving for hegemony, *i.e.,* for the conquest of territory, not so much directly

[1] *Die Neue Zeit,* 32nd year (1913-14), II, p. 909; *cf.* also 34th year (1915-16), II, p. 107 *et seq.*

for themselves as to weaken the adversary and undermine *his* hegemony. (Belgium is chiefly necessary to Germany as a base for operations against England; England needs Bagdad as a base for operations against Germany, etc.)

Kautsky refers especially—and repeatedly—to English writers who, he alleges, have given a purely political meaning to the word "imperialism" in the sense that Kautsky understands it. We take up the work by the Englishman Hobson, *Imperialism*, which appeared in 1902, and therein we read:

"The new imperialism differs from the older, first, in substituting for the ambition of a single growing empire the theory and the practice of competing empires, each motivated by similar lusts of political aggrandisement and commercial gain; secondly, in the dominance of financial or investing over mercantile interests." [2]

We see, therefore, that Kautsky is absolutely wrong in referring to English writers generally (unless he meant the vulgar English imperialist writers, or the avowed apologists for imperialism). We see that Kautsky, while claiming that he continues to defend Marxism, as a matter of fact takes a step backward compared with the *social-liberal* Hobson, who *more correctly* takes into account two "historically concrete" (Kautsky's definition is a mockery of historical concreteness) features of modern imperialism: 1) the competition between *several* imperialisms, and 2) the predominance of the financier over the merchant. If it were chiefly a question of the annexation of agrarian countries by industrial countries, the role of the merchant would be predominant.

Kautsky's definition is not only wrong and un-Marxian. It serves as a basis for a whole system of views which run counter to Marxian theory and Marxian practice all along the line. We shall refer to this again later. The argument about words which Kautsky raises as to whether the modern stage of capitalism should be called "imperialism" or "the stage of finance capital" is of no importance. Call it what you will, it matters little. The fact of the matter is that Kautsky detaches the politics of imperialism from its economics, speaks of annexations as being a policy "preferred"

[2] J. A. Hobson, *Imperialism—a Study*, London, 1902, p. 324.

by finance capital, and opposes to it another bourgeois policy which, he alleges, is possible on this very basis of finance capital. According to his argument, monopolies in economics are compatible with non-monopolistic, non-violent, non-annexationist methods in politics. According to his argument, the territorial division of the world, which was completed precisely during the period of finance capital, and which constitutes the basis of the present peculiar forms of rivalry between the biggest capitalist states, is compatible with a non-imperialist policy. The result is a slurring-over and a blunting of the most profound contradictions of the latest stage of capitalism, instead of an exposure of their depth; the result is bourgeois reformism instead of Marxism.

Kautsky enters into controversy with the German apologist of imperialism and annexations, Cunow, who clumsily and cynically argues that: imperialism is modern capitalism, the development of capitalism is inevitable and progressive; therefore imperialism is progressive; therefore, we should cringe before and eulogise it. This is something like the caricature of Russian Marxism which the Narodniki drew in 1894-95. They used to argue as follows: if the Marxists believe that capitalism is inevitable in Russia, that it is progressive, then they ought to open a public-house and begin to implant capitalism! Kautsky's reply to Cunow is as follows: imperialism is not modern capitalism. It is only one of the forms of the policy of modern capitalism. This policy we can and should fight; we can and should fight against imperialism, annexations, etc.

The reply seems quite plausible, but in effect it is a more subtle and more disguised (and therefore more dangerous) propaganda of conciliation with imperialism; for unless it strikes at the economic basis of the trusts and banks, the "struggle" against the policy of the trusts and banks reduces itself to bourgeois reformism and pacifism, to an innocent and benevolent expression of pious hopes. Kautsky's theory means refraining from mentioning existing contradictions, forgetting the most important of them, instead of revealing them in their full depth; it is a theory that has nothing in common with Marxism. Naturally, such a "theory" can only serve the purpose of advocating unity with the Cunows.

Kautsky writes: "from the purely economic point of view it is not impossible that capitalism will yet go through a new phase, that of the extension of the policy of the cartels to foreign policy, the phase of ultra-imperialism," [3] *i.e.,* of a super-imperialism, a union of world imperialisms and not struggles among imperialisms; a phase when wars shall cease under capitalism, a phase of "the joint exploitation of the world by internationally combined finance capital." [4]

We shall have to deal with this "theory of ultra-imperialism" later on in order to show in detail how definitely and utterly it departs from Marxism. In keeping with the plan of the present work, we shall examine the exact economic data on this question. Is "ultra-imperialism" possible "from the purely economic point of view" or is it ultra-nonsense?

If, by purely economic point of view a "pure" abstraction is meant, then all that can be said reduces itself to the following proposition: evolution is proceeding towards monopoly; therefore the trend is towards a single world monopoly, to a universal trust. This is indisputable, but it is also as completely meaningless as is the statement that "evolution is proceeding" towards the manufacture of foodstuffs in laboratories. In this sense the "theory" of ultra-imperialism is no less absurd than a "theory of ultra-agriculture" would be.

If, on the other hand, we are discussing the "purely economic" conditions of the epoch of finance capital as an historically concrete epoch which opened at the beginning of the twentieth century, then the best reply that one can make to the lifeless abstractions of "ultra-imperialism" (which serve an exclusively reactionary aim: that of diverting attention from the depth of *existing* antagonisms) is to contrast them with the concrete economic realities of present-day world economy. Kautsky's utterly meaningless talk about ultra-imperialism encourages, among other things, that profoundly mistaken idea which only brings grist to the mill of the apologists of imperialism, *viz.,* that the rule of finance capital *lessens* the

[3] *Die Neue Zeit,* 32nd year (1913-14), II, Sept. 11, 1914, p. 909; *cf.* also 34th year (1915-16), II, p. 107 *et seq.*
[4] *Die Neue Zeit,* 33rd year, II (April 30, 1915), p. 144.

unevenness and contradictions inherent in world economy, whereas in reality it *increases* them.

R. Calwer, in his little book, *An Introduction to World Economics*,[5] attempted to compile the main, purely economic, data required to understand in a concrete way the internal relations of world economy at the end of the nineteenth and beginning of the twentieth centuries. He divides the world into five "main economic areas," as follows: 1) Central Europe (the whole of Europe with the exception of Russia and Great Britain); 2) Great Britain; 3) Russia; 4) Eastern Asia; 5) America; he includes the colonies in the "areas" of the state to which they belong and "leaves out" a few countries not distributed according to areas, such as Persia, Afghanistan and Arabia in Asia; Morocco and Abyssinia in Africa, etc.

Here is a brief summary of the economic data he quotes on these regions:

	Area	Pop.	Transport		Trade		Industry		
PRINCIPAL ECONOMIC AREAS	MILLION SQ. KM.	MILLIONS	RAILWAYS (THOUS. KM.)	MERCANTILE FLEET (MILLION TONS)	IMPORTS AND EXPORTS (BILLION MARKS)	OUTPUT OF COAL (MILLION TONS)	OUTPUT OF PIG IRON (MILLION TONS)	NO. OF COTTON SPINDLES (MILLION)	
1) Central European	27.6 (23.6) [6]	388 (146)	204	8	41	251	15	26	
2) British	28.9 (28.6) [6]	398 (355)	140	11	25	249	9	51	
3) Russian	22	131	63	1	3	16	3	7	
4) East Asian	12	389	8	1	2	8	0.02	2	
5) American	30	148	379	6	14	245	14	19	

We notice three areas of highly developed capitalism with a high development of means of transport, of trade and of industry, the Central European, the British and the American areas. Among these are three states which dominate the world: Germany, Great Britain, the United States. Imperialist rivalry and the struggle between these countries have become very keen because Germany

[5] R. Calwer, *Einführung in die Weltwirtschaft*, Berlin, 1906.
[6] The figures in parentheses show the area and population of the colonies.

has only a restricted area and few colonies (the creation of "Central Europe" is still a matter for the future; it is being born in the midst of desperate struggles). For the moment the distinctive feature of Europe is political disintegration. In the British and American areas, on the other hand, political concentration is very highly developed, but there is a tremendous disparity between the immense colonies of the one and the insignificant colonies of the other. In the colonies, capitalism is only beginning to develop. The struggle for South America is becoming more and more acute.

There are two areas where capitalism is not strongly developed: Russia and Eastern Asia. In the former, the density of population is very low, in the latter it is very high; in the former political concentration is very high, in the latter it does not exist. The partition of China is only beginning, and the struggle between Japan, U.S.A., etc., in connection therewith is continually gaining in intensity.

Compare this reality, the vast diversity of economic and political conditions, the extreme disparity in the rate of development of the various countries, etc., and the violent struggles of the imperialist states, with Kautsky's silly little fable about "peaceful" ultra-imperialism. Is this not the reactionary attempt of a frightened philistine to hide from stern reality? Are not the international cartels which Kautsky imagines are the embryos of "ultra-imperialism" (with as much reason as one would have for describing the manufacture of tabloids in a laboratory as ultra-agriculture in embryo) an example of the division and the *redivision* of the world, the transition from peaceful division to non-peaceful division and *vice versa*? Is not American and other finance capital, which divided the whole world peacefully, with Germany's participation, for example, in the international rail syndicate, or in the international mercantile shipping trust, now engaged in *redividing* the world on the basis of a new relation of forces, which has been changed by methods *by no means* peaceful?

Finance capital and the trusts are increasing instead of diminishing the differences in the rate of development of the various parts of world economy. When the relation of forces is changed, how else, *under capitalism,* can the solution of contradictions be found, except by resorting to *violence?* Railway statistics [7] provide remarkably exact data on the different rates of development of capitalism and finance capital in world economy. In the last decades of imperialist development, the total length of railways has changed as follows:

RAILWAYS (*thousand kilometres*)

	1890	1913	INCREASE
Europe	224	346	122
U.S.A.	268	411	143
Colonies (total)	82 ⎤	210 ⎤	128 ⎤
Independent and semi-dependent states of Asia and America	⎬ 125 43 ⎦	⎬ 347 137 ⎦	⎬ 222 94 ⎦
Total	617	1,104	

Thus, the development of railways has been more rapid in the colonies and in the independent (and semi-dependent) states of Asia and America. Here, as we know, the finance capital of the four or five biggest capitalist states reigns undisputed. Two hundred thousand kilometres of new railways in the colonies and in the other countries of Asia and America represent more than 40,000,000,000 marks in capital, newly invested on particularly advantageous terms, with special guarantees of a good return and with profitable orders for steel works, etc., etc.

Capitalism is growing with the greatest rapidity in the colonies and in overseas countries. Among the latter, *new* imperialist powers are emerging (*e.g.,* Japan). The struggle of world imperialism is becoming more acute. The tribute levied by finance capital on the most profitable colonial and overseas enterprises is increasing. In sharing out this "booty," an exceptionally large part goes to countries which, as far as the development of productive forces is concerned, do not always stand at the top of the list. In the case

[7] *Statistisches Jahrbuch für das Deutsche Reich* (*Statistical Yearbook for the German Empire*), 1915, Appendix pp. 46, 47, *Archiv für Eisenbahnwesen* (*Railroad Archive*), 1892. Minor detailed figures for the distribution of railways among the colonies of the various countries in 1890 had to be estimated approximately.

of the biggest countries, considered with their colonies, the total
length of railways was as follows (in thousands of kilometres):

	1890	1913	INCREASE
U.S.A.	268	413	145
British Empire	107	208	101
Russia	32	78	46
Germany	43	68	25
France	41	63	22
Total	491	830	339

Thus, about 80 per cent of the total existing railways are concentrated in the hands of the five Great Powers. But the concentration of the *ownership* of these railways, of finance capital, is
much greater still: French and English millionaires, for example,
own an enormous amount of stocks and bonds in American, Russian and other railways.

Thanks to her colonies, Great Britain has increased the length
of "her" railways by 100,000 kilometres, four times as much as
Germany. And yet, it is well known that the development of productive forces in Germany, and especially the development of the
coal and iron industries, has been much more rapid during this
period than in England—not to mention France and Russia. In
1892, Germany produced 4,900,000 tons of pig iron and Great
Britain produced 6,800,000 tons; in 1912, Germany produced
17,600,000 tons and Great Britain 9,000,000 tons. Germany, therefore, had an overwhelming superiority over England in this respect.[8] We ask, is there *under capitalism* any means of removing
the disparity between the development of productive forces and
the accumulation of capital on the one side, and the division of
colonies and "spheres of influence" for finance capital on the other
side—other than by resorting to war?

[8] *Cf.* also Edgar Crummond, "The Economic Relation of the British and German
Empires," in *Journal of the Royal Statistical Society*, July 1914, p. 777, *et seq.*

CHAPTER VIII

The Parasitism and Decay
of Capitalism

WE have to examine yet another very important aspect of imperialism to which, usually, too little importance is attached in most of the arguments on this subject. One of the shortcomings of the Marxist Hilferding is that he takes a step backward compared with the non-Marxist Hobson. We refer to parasitism, which is a feature of imperialism.

As we have seen, the most deep-rooted economic foundation of imperialism is monopoly. This is capitalist monopoly, *i.e.,* monopoly which has grown out of capitalism and exists in the general environment of capitalism, commodity production and competition, and remains in permanent and insoluble contradiction to this general environment. Nevertheless, like all monopoly, this capitalist monopoly inevitably gives rise to a tendency to stagnation and decay. As monopoly prices become fixed, even temporarily, so the stimulus to technical and, consequently, to all progress, disappears to a certain extent, and to that extent, also, the *economic* possibility arises of deliberately retarding technical progress. For instance, in America, a certain Mr. Owens invented a machine which revolutionised the manufacture of bottles. The German bottle manufacturing cartel purchased Owens' patent, but pigeonholed it, refrained from utilising it. Certainly, monopoly under capitalism can never completely, and for a long period of time, eliminate competition in the world market (and this, by the by, is one of the reasons why the theory of ultra-imperialism is so absurd). Certainly the possibility of reducing cost of production and increasing profits by introducing technical improvements operates in the direction of change. Nevertheless, the *tendency* to stagnation and decay, which is the feature of monopoly, continues, and in certain branches of industry, in certain countries, for certain periods of time, it becomes predominant.

The monopoly of ownership of very extensive, rich or well-situated colonies, operates in the same direction.

Further, imperialism is an immense accumulation of money capital in a few countries, which, as we have seen, amounts to 100-150 billion francs in various securities. Hence the extraordinary growth of a class, or rather of a category, of *bondholders* (*rentiers*), *i.e.*, people who live by "clipping coupons," who take no part whatever in production, whose profession is idleness. The export of capital, one of the most essential economic bases of imperialism, still more completely isolates the *rentiers* from production and sets the seal of parasitism on the whole country that lives by the exploitation of the labour of several overseas countries and colonies.

"In 1893," writes Hobson, "the British capital invested abroad represented about 15 per cent of the total wealth of the United Kingdom."[1]

Let us remember that by 1915 this capital had increased about two and a half times.

"Aggressive imperialism," says Hobson further on, "which costs the taxpayer so dear, which is of so little value to the manufacturer and trader...is a source of great gain to the investor....The annual income Great Britain derives from commissions in her whole foreign and colonial trade, import and export, is estimated by Sir R. Giffen at £18,000,000 for 1899, taken at 2½ per cent, upon a turnover of £800,000,000."[2]

Great as this sum is, it does not explain the aggressive imperialism of Great Britain. This is explained by the 90 to 100 million pounds sterling income from "invested" capital, the income of the rentiers.

The income of the bondholders is *five times greater* than the income obtained from the foreign trade of the greatest "trading" country in the world. This is the essence of imperialism and imperialist parisitism.

For that reason the term, "rentier state" (*Rentnerstaat*), or

[1] *Op. cit.*, p. 59.—*Ed.*
[2] *Op. cit.*, pp. 62-3.—*Ed.*

usurer state, is passing into current use in the economic literature that deals with imperialism. The world has become divided into a handful of usurer states on the one side, and a vast majority of debtor states on the other.

"The premier place among foreign investments," says Schulze-Gaevernitz, "is held by those placed in politically dependent or closely allied countries. Great Britain grants loans to Egypt, Japan, China and South America. Her navy plays here the part of bailiff in case of necessity. Great Britain's political power protects her from the indignation of her debtors." [3]

Sartorius von Waltershausen in his book, *The National Economic System of Foreign Investments,* cites Holland as the model "rentier state" and points out that Great Britain and France have taken the same road.[4] Schilder believes that five industrial nations have become "pronounced creditor nations": Great Britain, France, Germany, Belgium and Switzerland. Holland does not appear on this list simply because she is "industrially less developed." [5] The United States is creditor only of the other American countries.

"Great Britain," says Schulze-Gaevernitz, "is gradually becoming transformed from an industrial state into a creditor state. Notwithstanding the absolute increase in industrial output and the export of manufactured goods, the relative importance of income from interest and dividends, issues of securities, commissions and speculation is on the increase in the whole of the national economy. In my opinion it is precisely this that forms the economic basis of imperialist ascendancy. The creditor is more permanently attached to the debtor than the seller is to the buyer." [6]

In regard to Germany, A. Lansburgh, the editor of *Die Bank,* in 1911, in an article entitled "Germany—a Rentier State," wrote the following:

[3] Schulze-Gaevernitz, *Britischer Imperialismus,* p. 320 *et seq.*

[4] Sartorius von Waltershausen, *Das volkswirtschaftliche System, etc. (The National Economic System, etc.),* Book IV, B. 1907.

[5] Schilder, *op. cit.,* pp. 392-93.

[6] Schulze-Gaevernitz, *op. cit.,* p. 122.—*Ed.*

"People in Germany are ready to sneer at the yearning to become rentiers that is observed among the people in France. But they forget that as far as the middle class is concerned the situation in Germany is becoming more and more like that in France." [7]

The rentier state is a state of parasitic, decaying capitalism, and this circumstance cannot fail to influence all the social-political conditions of the countries affected generally, and the two fundamental trends in the working closs movement, in particular. To demonstrate this in the clearest possible manner we will quote Hobson, who will be regarded as a more "reliable" witness, since he cannot be suspected of leanings towards "orthodox Marxism"; moreover, he is an Englishman who is very well acquainted with the situation in the country which is richest in colonies, in finance capital, and in imperialist experience.

With the Boer War fresh in his mind, Hobson describes the connection between imperialism and the interests of the "financiers," the growing profits from contracts, etc., and writes:

"While the directors of this definitely parasitic policy are capitalists, the same motives appeal to special classes of the workers. In many towns, most important trades are dependent upon government employment or contracts; the imperialism of the metal and shipbuilding centres is attributable in no small degree to this fact." [8]

In this writer's opinion there are two causes which weakened the older empires: 1) "economic parasitism," and 2) the formation of armies composed of subject races.

"There is first the habit of economic parasitism, by which the ruling state has used its provinces, colonies, and dependencies in order to enrich its ruling class and to bribe its lower classes into acquiescence." [9]

And we would add that the economic possibility of such corruption, whatever its form may be, requires high monopolist profits.
As for the second cause, Hobson writes:

[7] *Die Bank,* 1911, I, pp. 10-11.
[8] *Op. cit.,* p. 103.—*Ed.*
[9] *Op. cit.,* p. 205.

"One of the strangest symptoms of the blindness of imperialism is the reckless indifference with which Great Britain, France and other imperial nations are embarking on this perilous dependence. Great Britain has gone farthest. Most of the fighting by which we have won our Indian Empire has been done by natives; in India, as more recently in Egypt, great standing armies are placed under British commanders; almost all the fighting associated with our African dominions, except in the southern part, has been done for us by natives." [10]

Hobson gives the following economic appraisal of the prospect of the partition of China:

"The greater part of Western Europe might then assume the appearance and character already exhibited by tracts of country in the South of England, in the Riviera, and in the tourist-ridden or residential parts of Italy and Switzerland, little clusters of wealthy aristocrats drawing dividends and pensions from the Far East, with a somewhat larger group of professional retainers and tradesmen and a large body of personal servants and workers in the transport trade and in the final stages of production of the more perishable goods; all the main arterial industries would have disappeared, the staple foods and manufactures flowing in as tribute from Asia and Africa." [11]

"We have foreshadowed the possibility of even a larger alliance of Western States, a European federation of great powers which, so far from forwarding the cause of world civilisation, might introduce the gigantic peril of a Western parasitism, a group of advanced industrial nations, whose upper classes drew vast tribute from Asia and Africa, with which they supported great, tame masses of retainers, no longer engaged in the staple industries of agriculture and manufacture, but kept in the performance of personal or minor industrial services under the control of a new financial aristocracy. Let those who would scout such a theory as undeserving of consideration examine the economic and social condition of districts in Southern England today which are already reduced to this condition, and reflect upon the vast extension of such a system which might be rendered feasible by the subjection of China to the economic control of similar groups of financiers, investors, and political and business officials, draining the greatest potential reser-

[10] *Op. cit.*, p. 144.
[11] *Op. cit.*, p. 335.

voir of profit the world has ever known, in order to consume it in
Europe. The situation is far too complex, the play of world forces far
too incalculable, to render this or any other single interpretation of the
future very probable: but the influences which govern the imperialism
of Western Europe today are moving in this direction, and, unless
counteracted or diverted, make towards some such consummation." [12]

Hobson is quite right. *Unless* the forces of imperialism are counteracted they will lead precisely to what he has described. He correctly appraises the significance of a "United States of Europe" in
the present conditions of imperialism. He should have added, however, that, *even within* the working class movement, the opportunists, who are for the moment predominant in most countries,
are "working" systematically and undeviatingly in this very direction. Imperialism, which means the partition of the world, and the
exploitation of other countries besides China, which means high
monopoly profits for a handful of very rich countries, creates the
economic possibility of corrupting the upper strata of the proletariat, and thereby fosters, gives form to, and strengthens opportunism. However, we must not lose sight of the forces which
counteract imperialism in general, and opportunism in particular,
which, naturally, the social-liberal Hobson is unable to perceive.

The German opportunist, Gerhard Hildebrand, who was expelled
from the Party for defending imperialism, and who would today
make a leader of the so-called "Social-Democratic" Party of Germany, serves as a good supplement to Hobson by his advocacy of
a "United States of Western Europe" (without Russia) for the
purpose of "joint" action ... against the African Negroes, against
the "great Islamic movement," for the upkeep of a "powerful army
and navy," against a "Sino-Japanese coalition," etc. [13]

The description of "British imperialism" in Schulze-Gaevernitz's
book reveals the same parasitical traits. The national income of
Great Britain approximately doubled from 1865 to 1898, while the
income "from abroad" increased *ninefold* in the same period.
While the "merit" of imperialism is that it "trains the Negro to

[12] *Op. cit.,* pp. 385-86.
[13] Gerhard Hildebrand, *Die Erschütterung der Industrieherrschaft und des In-
dustriesozialismus,* Jena, 1910, p. 229 *et seq.*

habits of industry" (not without coercion of course...), the "danger" of imperialism is that:

"Europe...will shift the burden of physical toil—first agricultural and mining, then the more arduous toil in industry—on to the coloured races, and itself be content with the role of rentier, and in this way, perhaps, pave the way for the economic, and later, the political emancipation of the coloured races."

An increasing proportion of land in Great Britain is being taken out of cultivation and used for sport, for the diversion of the rich.

"Scotland," says Schulze-Gaevernitz, "is the most aristocratic playground in the world—it lives...on its past and on Mr. Carnegie."

On horse-racing and fox-hunting alone Britain annually spends £14,000,000. The number of rentiers in England is about one million. The percentage of the productively employed population to the total population is becoming smaller.

Year	POPULATION	NO. OF WORK-ERS IN BASIC INDUSTRIES (*millions*)	PER CENT OF TOTAL POPULATION
1851	17.9	4.1	23
1901	32.5	4.9	15

And in speaking of the British working class the bourgeois student of "British imperialism at the beginning of the twentieth century" is obliged to distinguish systematically between the *"upper stratum"* of the workers and the *"lower stratum of the proletariat proper."* The upper stratum furnishes the main body of members of co-operatives, of trade unions, of sporting clubs and of numerous religious sects. The electoral system, which in Great Britain is still *"sufficiently restricted to exclude the lower stratum of the proletariat proper,"* is adapted to their level!! In order to present the condition of the British working class in the best possible light, only this upper stratum—which constitutes only a *minority* of the proletariat—is generally spoken of. For instance, "the problem of unemployment is mainly a London problem and that of the lower

proletarian stratum, *which is of little political moment* for politicians."[14] It would be better to say: which is of little political
moment for the bourgeois politicians and the "socialist" opportunists.

Another special feature of imperialism, which is connected with
the facts we are describing, is the decline in emigration from imperialist countries, and the increase in immigration into these countries from the backward countries where lower wages are paid. As
Hobson observes, emigration from Great Britain has been declin-
ing since 1884. In that year the number of emigrants was 242,000,
while in 1900, the number was only 169,000. German emigration
reached the highest point between 1880 and 1890, with a total of
1,453,000 emigrants. In the course of the following two decades, it
fell to 544,000 and even to 341,000. On the other hand, there was
an increase in the number of workers entering Germany from
Austria, Italy, Russia and other countries. According to the 1907
census, there were 1,342,294 foreigners in Germany, of whom
440,800 were industrial workers and 257,329 were agricultural
workers.[15] In France, the workers employed in the mining industry
are, "in great part," foreigners: Polish, Italian and Spanish.[16] In the
United States, immigrants from Eastern and Southern Europe are
engaged in the most poorly paid occupations, while American
workers provide the highest percentage of overseers or of the better
paid workers.[17] Imperialism has the tendency to create privileged
sections even among the workers, and to detach them from the
main proletarian masses.

It must be observed that in Great Britain the tendency of imperialism to divide the workers, to encourage opportunism among
them and to cause temporary decay in the working class movement,
revealed itself much earlier than the end of the nineteenth and the
beginning of the twentieth centuries; for two important distinguishing features of imperialism were observed in Great Britain in the

---

[14] Schulze-Gaevernitz, *Britischer Imperialismus*, pp. 246, 301, 317, 323, 324, 361.
[15] *Statistik des Deutschen Reichs (Statistics of the German Empire)*, Vol. 211.
[16] Henger, *Die Kapitalsanlage der Franzosen (French Investments)*, Stuttgart, 1913.
[17] Hourwich, *Immigration and Labour*, New York, 1913.

middle of the nineteenth century, *viz.,* vast colonial possessions and a monopolist position in the world market. Marx and Engels systematically traced this relation between opportunism in the labour movement and the imperialist features of British capitalism for several decades. For example, on October 7, 1858, Engels wrote to Marx:

"The English proletariat is becoming more and more bourgeois, so that this most bourgeois of all nations is apparently aiming ultimately at the possession of a bourgeois aristocracy, and a bourgeois proletariat *as well as* a bourgeoisie. For a nation which exploits the whole world this is, of course, to a certain extent justifiable."

Almost a quarter of a century later, in a letter dated August 11, 1881, Engels speaks of "... the worst type of English trade unions which allow themselves to be led by men sold to, or at least, paid by the bourgeoisie."[18] In a letter to Kautsky, dated September 12, 1882, Engels wrote:

"You ask me what the English workers think about colonial policy? Well, exactly the same as they think about politics in general. There is no workers' party here, there are only Conservatives and Liberal-Radicals, and the workers merrily share the feast of England's monopoly of the colonies and the world market...."[19] (Engels expressed similar ideas in the press in his preface to the second edition of *The Condition of the Working Class in England,* which appeared in 1892.)

We thus see clearly the causes and effects. The causes are: 1) Exploitation of the whole world by this country. 2) Its monopolistic position in the world market. 3) Its colonial monopoly. The effects are: 1) A section of the British proletariat becomes bourgeois. 2) A section of the proletariat permits itself to be led by men sold to, or at least, paid by the bourgeoisie. The imperialism of the beginning of the twentieth century completed the division of the world among a handful of states, each of which today exploits (*i.e.,* draws super-profits from) a part of the world only a little

[18] Marx and Engels, *Selected Correspondence, 1846–1895,* International Publishers, New York, 1942, pp. 115–16, 399.—*Ed.*

[19] *Cf. Karl Kautsky, Sozialismus und Kolonialpolitik,* Berlin, 1907, p. 79; this pamphlet was written by Kautsky in those infinitely distant days when he was still a Marxist.

smaller than that which England exploited in 1858. Each of them, by means of trusts, cartels, finance capital, and debtor and creditor relations, occupies a monopoly position in the world market. Each of them enjoys to some degree a colonial monopoly. (We have seen that out of the total of 75,000,000 sq. km. which comprise the *whole* colonial world, 65,000,000 sq. km., or 86 per cent, belong to six great powers; 61,000,000 sq. km., or 81 per cent, belong to three powers.)

The distinctive feature of the present situation is the prevalence of economic and political conditions which could not but increase the irreconcilability between opportunism and the general and vital interests of the working class movement. Embryonic imperialism has grown into a dominant system; capitalist monopolies occupy first place in economics and politics; the division of the world has been completed. On the other hand, instead of an undisputed monopoly by Great Britain, we see a few imperialist powers contending for the right to share in this monopoly, and this struggle is characteristic of the whole period of the beginning of the twentieth century. Opportunism, therefore, cannot now triumph in the working class movement of any country for decades as it did in England in the second half of the nineteenth century. But, in a number of countries it has grown ripe, over-ripe, and rotten, and has become completely merged with bourgeois policy in the form of "social-chauvinism." [20]

[20] Russian social-chauvinism represented by Messrs. Potresov, Chkhenkeli, Maslov, etc., in its avowed form as well as in its tacit form, as represented by Messrs. Chkheidze, Skobelev, Axelrod, Martov, etc., also emerged from the Russian variety of opportunism, namely liquidationism.

CHAPTER IX

The Critique of Imperialism

By the critique of imperialism, in the broad sense of the term, we mean the attiude towards imperialist policy of the different classes of society as part of their general ideology.

The enormous dimensions of finance capital concentrated in a few hands and creating an extremely extensive and close network of ties and relationships which subordinate not only the small and medium, but also even the very small capitalists and small masters, on the one hand, and the intense struggle waged against other national state groups of financiers for the division of the world and domination over other countries, on the other hand, cause the wholesale transition of the possessing classes to the side of imperialism. The signs of the times are a "general" enthusiasm regarding its prospects, a passionate defence of imperialism, and every possible embellishment of its real nature. The imperialist ideology also penetrates the working class. There is no Chinese Wall between it and the other classes. The leaders of the so-called "Social-Democratic" Party of Germany are today justly called "social-imperialists," that is, socialists in words and imperialists in deeds; but as early as 1902, Hobson noted the existence of "Fabian imperialists" who belonged to the opportunist Fabian Society in England.

Bourgeois scholars and publicists usually come out in defence of imperialism in a somewhat veiled form, and obscure its complete domination and its profound roots; they strive to concentrate attention on partial and secondary details and do their very best to distract attention from the main issue by means of ridiculous schemes for "reform," such as police supervision of the trusts and banks, etc. Less frequently, cynical and frank imperialists speak out and are bold enough to admit the absurdity of the idea of reforming the fundamental features of imperialism.

We will give an example. The German imperialists attempt, in
the magazine *Archives of World Economy,* to follow the movements
for national emancipation in the colonies, particularly, of course,
in colonies other than those belonging to Germany. They note the
ferment and protest movements in India, the movement in Natal
(South Africa), the movement in the Dutch East Indies, etc. One
of them, commenting on an English report of the speeches delivered
at a conference of subject peoples and races, held on June 28-30,
1910, at which representatives of various peoples subject to foreign
domination in Africa, Asia and Europe were present, writes as
follows in appraising the speeches delivered at this conference:

"We are told that we must fight against imperialism; that the
dominant states should recognise the right of subject peoples to home
rule; that an international tribunal should supervise the fulfilment of
treaties concluded between the great powers and weak peoples. One
does not get any further than the expression of these pious wishes. We
see no trace of understanding of the fact that imperialism is indis-
solubly bound up with capitalism in its present form" (!!) "and therefore also no trace of the realisation that an open struggle against
imperialism would be hopeless, unless, perhaps, the fight is confined to
protests against certain of its especially abhorrent excesses." [1]

Since the reform of the basis of imperialism is a deception, a
"pious wish," since the bourgeois representatives of the oppressed
nations go no "further" forward, the bourgeois representatives of
the oppressing nation go "further" *backward,* to servility, towards
imperialism, concealed by the cloak of "science." "Logic," indeed!
The question as to whether it is possible to reform the basis of
imperialism, whether to go forward to the accentuation and deepening of the antagonisms which it engenders, or backwards, towards
allaying these antagonisms, is a fundamental question in the
critique of imperialism. As a consequence of the fact that the
political features of imperialism are reaction all along the line,
and increased national oppression, resulting from the oppression
of the financial oligarchy and the elimination of free competition,
a petty-bourgeois—democratic opposition has been rising against
imperialism in almost all imperialist countries since the beginning

[1] *Weltwirtschaftliches Archiv (Archives of World Economy),* Vol. II, pp. 194-95.

of the twentieth century. And the desertion of Kautsky and of the broad international Kautskyan trend from Marxism is displayed in the very fact that Kautsky not only did not trouble to oppose, not only was unable to oppose this petty-bourgeois reformist opposition, which is really reactionary in its economic basis, but in practice actually became merged with it.

In the United States, the imperialist war waged against Spain in 1898 stirred up the opposition of the "anti-imperialists," the last of the Mohicans of bourgeois democracy. They declared this war to be "criminal"; they denounced the annexation of foreign territories as being a violation of the Constitution, and denounced the "Jingo treachery" by means of which Aguinaldo, leader of the native Filipinos, was deceived (the Americans promised him the independence of his country, but later they landed troops and annexed it). They quoted the words of Lincoln:

"When the white man governs himself, that is self-government; but when he governs himself and also governs another man, that is more than self-government—that is despotism." [2]

But while all this criticism shrank from recognising the indissoluble bond between imperialism and the trusts, and, therefore, between imperialism and the very foundations of capitalism; while it shrank from joining up with the forces engendered by large-scale capitalism and its development—it remained a "pious wish."

This is also, in the main, the attitude of Hobson in his criticism of imperialism. Hobson anticipated Kautsky in protesting against the "inevitability of imperialism" argument, and in urging the need to raise the consuming capacity of the "people" (under capitalism!). The petty-bourgeois point of view in the critique of imperialism, the domination of the banks, the financial oligarchy, etc., is that adopted by the authors we have often quoted, such as Agahd, A. Lansburgh, L. Eschwege; and among French writers, Victor Bérard, author of a superficial book entitled *England and Imperialism* which appeared in 1900. All these authors, who make

[2] Quoted by Patouillet, *L'impérialisme américain*, Dijon, 1904, p. 272. (From speech "On the Repeal of the Missouri Compromise," at Peoria, Illinois, October 16, 1854.—*Ed.*)

no claim to be Marxists, contrast imperialism with free competition and democracy; they condemn the Bagdad railway scheme as leading to disputes and war, utter "pious wishes" for peace, etc. This applies also to the compiler of international stock and share issue statistics, A. Neymarck, who, after calculating the hundreds of billions of francs representing "international" securities, exclaimed in 1912: "Is it possible to believe that peace may be disturbed... that, in the face of these enormous figures, anyone would risk starting a war?" [3]

Such simplicity of mind on the part of the bourgeois economists is not surprising. Besides, *it is in their interest* to pretend to be so naive and to talk "seriously" about peace under imperialism. But what remains of Kautsky's Marxism, when, in 1914-15-16, he takes up the same attitude as the bourgeois reformists and affirms that "everybody is agreed" (imperialists, pseudo-socialists and social-pacifists) as regards peace? Instead of an analysis of imperialism and an exposure of the depths of its contradictions, we have nothing but a reformist "pious wish" to wave it aside, to evade it.

Here is an example of Kautsky's economic criticism of imperialism. He takes the statistics of the British export and import trade with Egypt for 1872 and 1912. These statistics show that this export and import trade has developed more slowly than British foreign trade as a whole. From this Kautsky concludes that:

> "We have no reason to suppose that British trade with Egypt would have been less developed simply as a result of the mere operation of economic factors, without military occupation.... The urge of the present-day states to expand...can be best promoted, not by the violent methods of imperialism, but by peaceful democracy." [4]

This argument, which is repeated in every key by Kautsky's Russian armour-bearer (and Russian protector of the social-chauvinists), Mr. Spectator, represents the basis of Kautskyan criticism of imperialism and that is why we must deal with it in greater detail. We will begin with a quotation from Hilferding, whose

[3] *Bulletin de l'Institut International de Statistique*, Vol. XIX, Book II, p. 225.
[4] Karl Kautsky, *Nationalstaat, imperialistischer Staat und Staatenbund* (*National State, Imperialist State and Union of States*), Nuremberg, 1915, pp. 72, 70.

conclusions, as Kautsky on many occasions, and notably in April 1915, declared, have been "unanimously adopted by all socialist theoreticians."

"It is not the business of the proletariat," writes Hilferding, "to contrast the more progressive capitalist policy with that of the now by-gone era of free trade and of hostility towards the state. The reply of the proletariat to the economic policy of finance capital, to imperialism, cannot be free trade, but socialism. The aim of proletarian policy cannot now be the ideal of restoring free competition—which has now become a reactionary ideal—but the complete abolition of competition by the vanquishment of capitalism." [5]

Kautsky departed from Marxism by advocating what is, in the period of finance capital, a "reactionary ideal," "peaceful democracy," "the mere operation of economic factors," for *objectively* this ideal drags us back from monopoly capitalism to the non-monopolist stage, and is a reformist swindle.

Trade with Egypt (or with any other colony or semi-colony) "would have grown more" *without* military occupation, without imperialism, and without finance capital. What does this mean? That capitalism would develop more rapidly if free competition were not restricted by monopolies in general, by the "connections" or the yoke (*i.e.,* also the monopoly) of finance capital, or by the monopolist possession of colonies by certain countries?

Kautsky's argument can have no other meaning; and *this* "meaning" is meaningless. But suppose, for the sake of argument, free competition, without any sort of monopoly, *would* develop capitalism and trade more rapidly. Is it not a fact that the more rapidly trade and capitalism develop, the greater is the concentration of production and capital which *gives rise* to monopoly? And monopolies have *already* come into being—precisely *out of* free competition! Even if monopolies have now begun to retard progress, it is not an argument in favour of free competition, which has become impossible since it gave rise to monopoly.

Whichever way one turns Kautsky's argument, one will find nothing in it except reaction and bourgeois reformism.

[5] Hilferding, *op. cit.,* pp. 471-72.

Even if we modify this argument and say, as Spectator says, that the trade of the British colonies with the mother country is now developing more slowly than their trade with other countries, it does not save Kautsky; for it is *also* monopoly and imperialism that is beating Great Britain, only it is the monopoly and imperialism of another country (America, Germany). It is known that the cartels have given rise to a new and peculiar form of protective tariffs, *i.e.*, goods suitable for export are protected (Engels noted this in Vol. III of *Capital*). It is known, too, that the cartels and finance capital have a system peculiar to themselves, that of "exporting goods at cut-rate prices," or "dumping," as the English call it: within a given country the cartel sells its goods at a high price fixed by monopoly; abroad it sells them at a much lower price to undercut the competitor, to enlarge its own production to the utmost, etc. If Germany's trade with the British colonies is developing more rapidly than that of Great Britain with the same colonies, it only proves that German imperialism is younger, stronger and better organised than British imperialism, is superior to it. But this by no means proves the "superiority" of free trade, for it is not free trade fighting against protection and colonial dependence, but two rival imperialisms, two monopolies, two groups of finance capital that are fighting. The superiority of German imperialism over British imperialism is stronger than the wall of colonial frontiers or of protective tariffs. To use this as an argument *in favour* of free trade and "peaceful democracy" is banal, is to forget the essential features and qualities of imperialism, to substitute petty-bourgeois reformism for Marxism.

It is interesting to note that even the bourgeois economist, A. Lansburgh, whose criticism of imperialism is as petty-bourgeois as Kautsky's, nevertheless got closer to a more scientific study of trade statistics. He did not compare merely one country, chosen at random, and a colony, with the other countries; he examined the export trade of an imperialist country: 1) with countries which are financially dependent upon it, which borrow money from it; and 2) with countries which are financially independent. He obtained the following results:

EXPORT TRADE OF GERMANY (*million marks*)

COUNTRIES FINANCIALLY DEPENDENT ON GERMANY	1889	1908	PER CENT INCREASE
Rumania	48.2	70.8	47
Portugal	19.0	32.8	73
Argentina	60.7	147.0	143
Brazil	48.7	84.5	73
Chile	28.3	52.4	85
Turkey	29.9	64.0	114
Total	234.8	451.5	92
COUNTRIES FINANCIALLY INDEPENDENT OF GERMANY			
Great Britain	651.8	997.4	53
France	210.2	437.9	108
Belgium	137.2	322.8	135
Switzerland	177.4	401.1	127
Australia	21.2	64.5	205
Dutch East Indies	8.8	40.7	363
Total	1,206.6	2,264.4	87

Lansburgh did not draw *conclusions* and therefore, strangely enough, failed to observe that *if* the figures prove anything at all, they prove that *he is wrong,* for the exports to countries financially dependent on Germany have grown *more rapidly,* if only slightly, than those to the countries which are financially independent. (We emphasise the "if," for Lansburgh's figures are far from complete.)

Tracing the connection between export trade and loans, Lansburgh writes:

"In 1890-91, a Rumanian loan was floated through the German banks, which had already in previous years made advances on this loan. The loan was used chiefly for purchases of railway materials in Germany. In 1891 German exports to Rumania amounted to 55,000,000 marks. The following year they fell to 39,400,000 marks; then with fluctuations, to 25,400,000 in 1900. Only in very recent years have they regained the level of 1891, thanks to several new loans.

"German exports to Portugal rose, following the loans of 1888-89, **to**

21,100,000 (1890); then fell, in the two following years, to 16,200,000 and 7,400,000; and only regained their former level in 1903.

"German trade with the Argentine is still more striking. Following the loans floated in 1888 and 1890, German exports to the Argentine reached, in 1889, 60,700,000 marks. Two years later they only reached 18,600,000 marks, that is to say, less than one-third of the previous figure. It was not until 1901 that they regained and surpassed the level of 1889, and then only as a result of new loans floated by the state and by municipalities, with advances to build power stations, and with other credit operations.

"Exports to Chile rose to 45,200,000 marks in 1892, after the loan negotiated in 1889. The following year they fell to 22,500,000 marks. A new Chilean loan floated by the German banks in 1906 was followed by a rise of exports in 1907 to 84,700,000 marks, only to fall again to 52,400,000 marks in 1908." [6]

From all these facts Lansburgh draws the amusing petty-bourgeois moral of how unstable and irregular export trade is when it is bound up with loans, how bad it is to invest capital abroad instead of "naturally" and "harmoniously" developing home industry, how "costly" is the *backsheesh* that Krupp has to pay in floating foreign loans, etc.! But the facts are clear. The increase in exports is *closely* connected with the swindling tricks of finance capital, which is not concerned with bourgeois morality, but with skinning the ox twice—first, it pockets the profits from the loan; then it pockets other profits from the *same* loan which the borrower uses to make purchases from Krupp, or to purchase railway material from the Steel Syndicate, etc.

We repeat that we do not by any means consider Lansburgh's figures to be perfect. But we had to quote them because they are more scientific than Kautsky's and Spectator's, and because Lansburgh showed the correct way of approaching the question. In discussing the significance of finance capital in regard to exports, etc., one must be able to single out the connection of exports especially and solely with the tricks of the financiers, especially and solely with the sale of goods by cartels, etc. Simply to compare colonies with non-colonies, one imperialism with another imperialism,

---

[6] *Die Bank,* 1909, Vol. II, pp. 826-27.

one semi-colony or colony (Egypt) with all other countries, is to evade and to tone down the very *essence* of the question.

Kautsky's theoretical critique of imperialism has nothing in common with Marxism and serves no other purpose than as a preamble to propaganda for peace and unity with the opportunists and the social-chauvinists, precisely for the reason that it evades and obscures the very profound and radical contradictions of imperialism: the contradictions between monopoly and free competition that exists side by side with it, betwen the gigantic "operations" (and gigantic profits) of finance capital and "honest" trade in the free market, the contradictions between cartels and trusts, on the one hand, and non-cartelised industry, on the other, etc.

The notorious theory of "ultra-imperialism," invented by Kautsky, is equally reactionary. Compare his arguments on this subject in 1915, with Hobson's arguments in 1902.

Kautsky:

"Cannot the present imperialist policy be supplanted by a new, ultra-imperialist policy, which will introduce the common exploitation of the world by internationally united finance capital in place of the mutual rivalries of national finance capital? Such a new phase of capitalism is at any rate conceivable. Can it be achieved? Sufficient premises are still lacking to enable us to answer this question." [7]

Hobson:

"Christendom thus laid out in a few great federal empires, each with a retinue of uncivilised dependencies, seems to many the most legitimate development of present tendencies, and one which would offer the best hope of permanent peace on an assured basis of inter-imperialism." [8]

Kautsky called ultra-imperialism or super-imperialism what Hobson, thirteen years earlier, described as inter-imperialism. Except for coining a new and clever word, by replacing one Latin prefix by another, the only progress Kautsky has made in the sphere of "scientific" thought is that he has labelled as Marxism what Hobson, in effect, described as the cant of English parsons. After the Anglo-Boer War it was quite natural for this worthy caste

[7] *Die Neue Zeit*, April 30, 1915, p. 144.
[8] Hobson, *op. cit.*, p. 351.

to exert every effort to *console* the British middle class and the workers who had lost many of their relatives on the battlefields of South Africa and who were obliged to pay higher taxes in order to guarantee still higher profits for the British financiers. And what better consolation could there be than the theory that imperialism is not so bad; that it stands close to inter- (or ultra-) imperialism, which can ensure permanent peace? No matter what the good intentions of the English parsons, or of sentimental Kautsky, may have been, the only objective, *i.e.,* real, social significance Kautsky's "theory" can have, is that of a most reactionary method of consoling the masses with hopes of permanent peace being possible under capitalism, distracting their attention from the sharp antagonisms and acute problems of the present era, and directing it towards illusory prospects of an imaginary "ultra-imperialism" of the future. Deception of the masses—there is nothing but this in Kautsky's "Marxian" theory.

Indeed, it is enough to compare well-known and indisputable facts to become convinced of the utter falsity of the prospects which Kautsky tries to conjure up before the German workers (and the workers of all lands). Let us consider India, Indo-China and China. It is known that these three colonial and semi-colonial countries, inhabited by six to seven hundred million human beings, are subjected to the exploitation of the finance capital of several imperialist states: Great Britain, France, Japan, the U.S.A., etc. We will asume that these imperialist countries form alliances against one another in order to protect and extend their possessions, their interests and their "spheres of influence" in these Asiatic states; these alliances will be "inter-imperialist," or "ultra-imperialist" alliances. We will assume that *all* the imperialist countries conclude an alliance for the "peaceful" division of these parts of Asia; this alliance would be an alliance of "internationally united finance capital." As a matter of fact, alliances of this kind have been made in the twentieth century, notably with regard to China. We ask, is it "conceivable," assuming that the capitalist system remains intact—and this is precisely the assumption that Kautsky does make—that such alliances would be more than temporary, that they would eliminate friction, conflicts and struggle in all and every possible form?

This question need only be stated clearly enough to make it impossible for any other reply to be given than that in the negative; for there can be *no* other conceivable basis under capitalism for the division of spheres of influence, of interests, of colonies, etc., than a calculation of the *strength* of the participants in the division, their general economic, financial, military strength, etc. And the strength of these participants in the division does not change to an equal degree, for under capitalism the development of different undertakings, trusts, branches of industry, or countries cannot be *even*. Half a century ago, Germany was a miserable, insignificant country, as far as its capitalist strength was concerned, compared with the strength of England at that time. Japan was similarly insignificant compared with Russia. Is it "conceivable" that in ten or twenty years' time the relative strength of the imperialist powers will have remained *un*changed? Absolutely inconceivable.

Therefore, in the realities of the capitalist system, and not in the banal philistine fantasies of English parsons, or of the German "Marxist," Kautsky, "inter-imperialist" or "ultra-imperialist" alliances, no matter what form they may assume, whether of one imperialist coalition against another, or of a general alliance embracing *all* the imperialist powers, are *inevitably* nothing more than a "truce" in periods between wars. Peaceful alliances prepare the ground for wars, and in their turn grow out of wars; the one is the condition for the other, giving rise to alternating forms of peaceful and non-peaceful struggle out of *one and the same* basis of imperialist connections and the relations between world economics and world politics. But in order to pacify the workers and to reconcile them with the social-chauvinists who have deserted to the side of the bourgeoisie, wise Kautsky *separates* one link of a single chain from the other, separates the present peaceful (and ultra-imperialist, nay, ultra-ultra-imperialist) alliance of *all* the powers for the "pacification" of China (remember the suppression of the Boxer Rebellion) from the non-peaceful conflict of tomorrow, which will prepare the ground for another "peaceful" general alliance for the partition, say, of Turkey, on the day after tomorrow, etc., etc. Instead of showing the vital connection between periods of imperialist peace and periods of imperialist war, Kautsky puts before the workers a lifeless abstraction solely in order to reconcile them to their lifeless leaders.

An American writer, Hill, in his *History of Diplomacy in the International Development of Europe*,[9] points out in his preface the following periods of contemporary diplomatic history: 1) The era of revolution; 2) The constitutional movement; 3) The present era of "commercial imperialism." Another writer divides the history of Great Britain's foreign policy since 1870 into four periods: 1) The first Asiatic period (that of the struggle against Russia's advance in Central Asia towards India); 2) The African period (approximately 1885-1902): that of struggles against France for the partition of Africa (the Fashoda incident of 1898 which brought France within a hair's breadth of war with Great Britain); 3) The second Asiatic period (alliance with Japan against Russia), and 4) The European period, chiefly anti-German.[10] "The political skirmishes of outposts take place on the financial field," wrote Riesser, the banker, in 1905, in showing how French finance capital operating in Italy was preparing the way for a political alliance of these countries, and how a conflict was developing between Great Britain and Germany over Persia, between all the European capitalists over Chinese loans, etc. Behold, the living reality of peaceful "ultra-imperialist" alliances in their indissoluble connection with ordinary imperialist conflicts!

Kautsky's toning down of the deepest contradictions of imperialism, which inevitably becomes the embellishment of imperialism, leaves its traces in this writer's criticism of the political features of imperialism. Imperialism is the epoch of finance capital and of monopolies, which introduce everywhere the striving for domination, not for freedom. The result of these tendencies is reaction all along the line, whatever the political system, and an extreme intensification of existing antagonisms in this domain also. Par-

---

[9] David Jayne Hill, *A History of Diplomacy in the International Development of Europe*, Vol. I, p. x.

[10] Schilder, *op. cit.*, Vol. I, p. 178.

ticularly acute becomes the yoke of national oppression and the striving for annexations, *i.e.*, the violation of national independence (for annexation is nothing but the violation of the right of nations to self-determination). Hilferding justly draws attention to the connection between imperialism and the growth of national oppression.

"In the newly opened up countries themselves," he writes, "the capitalism imported into them intensifies contradictions and excites the constantly growing resistance against the intruders of the peoples who are awakening to national consciousness. This resistance can easily become transformed into dangerous measures directed against foreign capital. The old social relations become completely revolutionised. The age-long agrarian incrustation of 'nations without a history' is blasted away, and they are drawn into the capitalist whirlpool. Capitalism itself gradually procures for the vanquished the means and resources for their emancipation and they set out to achieve the same goal which once seemed highest to the European nations: the creation of a united national state as a means to economic and cultural freedom. This movement for national independence threatens European capital just in its most valuable and most promising fields of exploitation, and European capital can maintain its domination only by continually increasing its means of exerting violence." [11]

To this must be added that it is not only in newly opened up countries, but also in the old, that imperialism is leading to annexation, to increased national oppression, and, consequently, also to increasing resistance. While opposing the intensification of political reaction caused by imperialism, Kautsky obscures the question, which has become very serious, of the impossibility of unity with the opportunists in the epoch of imperialism. While objecting to annexations, he presents his objections in a form that will be most acceptable and least offensive to the opportunists. He addresses himself to a German audience, yet he obscures the most topical and important point, for instance, the annexation by Germany of Alsace-Lorraine. In order to appraise this "lapse of mind" of Kautsky's we will take the following example. Let us suppose that a Japanese

[11] Hilferding, *op. cit.*, p. 406.

is condemning the annexation of the Philippine Islands by the Americans. Will many believe that he is doing so because he has a horror of annexations as such, and not because he himself has a desire to annex the Philippines? And shall we not be constrained to admit that the "fight" the Japanese are waging against annexations can be regarded as being sincere and politically honest only if he fights against the annexation of Korea by Japan, and urges freedom for Korea to secede from Japan?

Kautsky's theoretical analysis of imperialism, as well as his economic and political criticism of imperialism, are permeated *through and through* with a spirit, absolutely irreconcilable with Marxism, of obscuring and glossing over the most profound contradictions of imperialism and with a striving to preserve the crumbling unity with opportunism in the European labour movement at all costs.

CHAPTER X

The Place of Imperialism
in History

WE have seen that the economic quintessence of imperialism is monopoly capitalism. This very fact determines its place in history, for monopoly that grew up on the basis of free competition, and precisely out of free competition, is the transition from the capitalist system to a higher social-economic order. We must take special note of the four principal forms of monopoly, or the four principal manifestations of monopoly capitalism, which are characteristic of the epoch under review.

Firstly, monopoly arose out of the concentration of production at a very advanced stage of development. This refers to the monopolist capitalist combines, cartels, syndicates and trusts. We have seen the important part that these play in modern economic life. At the beginning of the twentieth century, monopolies acquired complete supremacy in the advanced countries. And although the first steps towards the formation of the cartels were first taken by countries enjoying the protection of high tariffs (Germany, America), Great Britain, with her system of free trade, was not far behind in revealing the same basic phenomenon, namely, the birth of monopoly out of the concentration of production.

Secondly, monopolies have accelerated the capture of the most important sources of raw materials, especially for the coal and iron industries, which are the basic and most highly cartelised industries in capitalist society. The monopoly of the most important sources of raw materials has enormously increased the power of big capital, and has sharpened the antagonism between cartelised and non-cartelised industry.

Thirdly, monopoly has sprung from the banks. The banks have developed from modest intermediary enterprises into the monopolists of finance capital. Some three or five of the biggest banks in each of the foremost capitalist countries have achieved the "personal union" of industrial and bank capital, and have concentrated in their hands the disposal of thousands upon thousands of millions which form the greater part of the capital and income of entire countries. A financial oligarchy, which throws a close net of relations of dependence over all the economic and political institutions of contemporary bourgeois society without exception— such is the most striking manifestation of this monopoly.

Fourthly, monopoly has grown out of colonial policy. To the numerous "old" motives of colonial policy, finance capital has added the struggle for the sources of raw materials, for the export of capital, for "spheres of influence," *i.e.,* for spheres for profitable deals, concessions, monopolist profits and so on; in fine, for economic territory in general. When the colonies of the European powers in Africa, for instance, comprised only one-tenth of that territory (as was the case in 1876), colonial policy was able to develop by methods other than those of monopoly—by the "free grabbing" of territories, so to speak. But when nine-tenths of Africa had been seized (approximately by 1900), when the whole world had been divided up, there was inevitably ushered in a period of colonial monopoly and, consequently, a period of particularly intense struggle for the division and the redivision of the world.

The extent to which monopolist capital has intensified all the contradictions of capitalism is generally known. It is sufficient to mention the high cost of living and the oppression of the cartels. This intensification of contradictions constitutes the most powerful driving force of the transitional period of history, which began from the time of the definite victory of world finance capital.

Monopolies, oligarchy, the striving for domination instead of the striving for liberty, the exploitation of an increasing number of small or weak nations by an extremely small group of the richest or most powerful nations—all these have given birth to those distinctive characteristics of imperialism which compel us to define it as parasitic or decaying capitalism. More and more prominently there emerges, as one of the tendencies of imperialism, the creation of the "bondholding" (rentier) state, the usurer state, in which the bourgeoisie lives on the proceeds of capital exports and by "clipping coupons." It would be a mistake to believe that this tendency to decay precludes the possibility of the rapid growth of capitalism. It does not. In the epoch of imperialism, certain branches of industry, certain strata of the bourgeoisie and certain countries betray, to a more or less degree, one or other of these tendencies. On the whole, capitalism is growing far more rapidly than before. But this growth is not only becoming more and more uneven in general; its unevenness also manifests itself, in particular, in the decay of the countries which are richest in capital (such as England).

In regard to the rapidity of Germany's economic development, Riesser, the author of the book on the big German banks, states:

"The progress of the preceding period (1848-70), which had not been exactly slow, stood in about the same ratio to the rapidity with which the whole of Germany's national economy, and with it German banking, progressed during this period (1870-1905) as the mail coach of the Holy Roman Empire of the German nation stood to the speed of the present-day automobile...which in whizzing past, it must be said, often endangers not only innocent pedestrians in its path, but also the occupants of the car."[1]

In its turn, this finance capital which has grown so rapidly is not unwilling (precisely because it has grown so quickly) to pass on to a more "tranquil" possession of colonies which have to be seized—and not only by peaceful methods—from richer nations. In the United States, economic development in the last decades has been even more rapid than in Germany, and *for this very reason* the parasitic character of modern American capitalism has stood out with particular prominence. On the other hand, a comparison of, say, the republican American bourgeoisie with the monarchist Japanese or German bourgeoisie shows that the most pronounced political distinctions diminish to an extreme degree in the epoch of imperialism—not because they are unimportant in general, but because in all these cases we are discussing a bourgeoisie which has definite features of parasitism.

[1] Riesser, *op. cit.*, third ed., p. 354.—*Ed.*

The receipt of high monopoly profits by the capitalists in one of the numerous branches of industry, in one of numerous countries, etc., makes it economically possible for them to corrupt certain sections of the working class, and for a time a fairly considerable minority, and win them to the side of the bourgeoisie of a given industry or nation against all the others. The intensification of antagonisms between imperialist nations for the division of the world increases this striving. And so there is created that bond between imperialism and opportunism, which revealed itself first and most clearly in England, owing to the fact that certain features of imperialist development were observable there much earlier than in other countries.

Some writers, L. Martov, for example, try to evade the fact that there is a connection between imperialism and opportunism in the labour movement—which is particularly striking at the present time—by resorting to "official optimistic" arguments (à la Kautsky and Huysmans) like the following: the cause of the opponents of capitalism would be hopeless if it were precisely progressive capitalism that led to the increase of opportunism, or, if it were precisely the best paid workers who were inclined towards opportunism, etc. We must have no illusion regarding "optimism" of this kind. It is optimism in regard to opportunism; it is optimism which serves to conceal opportunism. As a matter of fact the extraordinary rapidity and the particularly revolting character of the development of opportunism is by no means a guarantee that its victory will be durable: the rapid growth of a malignant abscess on a healthy body only causes it to burst more quickly and thus to relieve the body of it. The most dangerous people of all in this respect are those who do not wish to understand that the fight against imperialism is a sham and humbug unless it is inseparably bound up with the fight against opportunism.

From all that has been said in this book on the economic nature of imperialism, it follows that we must define it as capitalism in transition, or, more precisely, as moribund capitalism. It is very instructive in this respect to note that the bourgeois economists, in describing modern capitalism, frequently employ terms like "interlocking," "absence of isolation," etc.; "in conformity with their functions and course of development," banks are "not purely private business enterprises; they are more and more outgrowing the sphere of purely private business regulation." And this very Riesser, who uttered the words just quoted, declares with all seriousness that the "prophecy" of the Marxists concerning "socialisation" has "not come true"!

What then does this word "interlocking" express? It merely expresses the most striking feature of the process going on before our eyes. It shows that the observer counts the separate trees, but cannot see the wood. It slavishly copies the superficial, the fortuitous, the chaotic. It reveals the observer as one who is overwhelmed by the mass of raw material and is utterly incapable of appreciating its meaning and importance. Ownership of shares and relations between owners of private property "interlock in a haphazard way." But the underlying factor of this interlocking, its very base, is the changing social relations of production. When a big enterprise assumes gigantic proportions, and, on the basis of exact computation of mass data, organises according to plan the supply of primary raw materials to the extent of two-thirds, or three-fourths of all that is necessary for tens of millions of people; when the raw materials are transported to the most suitable place of production, sometimes hundreds or thousands of miles away, in a systematic and organised manner; when a single centre directs all the successive stages of work right up to the manufacture of numerous varieties of finished articles; when these products are distributed according to a single plan among tens and hundreds of millions of consumers (as in the case of the distribution of oil in America and Germany by the American "oil trust")—then it becomes evident that we have socialisation of production, and not mere "interlocking"; that private economic relations and private property relations constitute a shell which is no longer suitable for its contents, a shell which must inevitably begin to decay if its destruction be delayed by artificial means; a shell which may continue in a state of decay for a fairly long period (particularly if the cure of the opportunist abscess is protracted), but which will inevitably be removed.

The enthusiastic admirer of German imperialism, Schulze-Gaevernitz, exclaims:

"Once the supreme management of the German banks has been entrusted to the hands of a dozen persons, their activity is even today more significant for the public good than that of the majority of the Ministers of State." (The "interlocking" of bankers, ministers, magnates of industry and rentiers is here conveniently forgotten.)... "If we conceive of the tendencies of development which we have noted as realised to the utmost: the money capital of the nation united in the banks; the banks themselves combined into cartels; the investment capital of the nation cast in the shape of securities, then the brilliant forecast of Saint-Simon will be fulfilled: 'The present anarchy of production caused by the fact that economic relations are developing without uniform regulation must make way for organisation in production. Production will no longer be shaped by isolated manufacturers, independent of each other and ignorant of man's economic needs, but by a social institution. A central body of management, being able to survey the large fields of social economy from a more elevated point of view, will regulate it for the benefit of the whole of society, will be able to put the means of production into suitable hands, and above all will take care that there be constant harmony between production and consumption. Institutions already exist which have assumed as part of their task a certain organisation of economic labour: the banks.' The fulfilment of the forecasts of Saint-Simon still lies in the future, but we are on the way to its fulfilment—Marxism, different from what Marx imagined, but different only in form." [2]

A crushing "refutation" of Marx, indeed! It is a retreat from Marx's precise, scientific analysis to Saint-Simon's guesswork, the guesswork of a genius, but guesswork all the same.

January–July, 1916.

[2] Schulze-Gaevernitz, in *Grundriss der Socialökonomik*, pp. 145-46.